*FOR ANNE-LISS,
AGAIN*

# THE KOREAN PIPELINE

## RAYMOND FLANDERS

PublishAmerica
Baltimore

© 2009 by Raymond Flanders.
All rights reserved. No part of this book may be reproduced, stored in a retrieval system or transmitted in any form or by any means without the prior written permission of the publishers, except by a reviewer who may quote brief passages in a review to be printed in a newspaper, magazine or journal.

First printing

PublishAmerica has allowed this work to remain exactly as the author intended, verbatim, without editorial input.

ISBN: 978-1-61582-196-9
PUBLISHED BY PUBLISHAMERICA, LLLP
www.publishamerica.com
Baltimore

Printed in the United States of America

THIS BOOK IS DEDICATED TO

THE ENLISTED MEN
WHO FOUGHT AND DIED DURING
THE KOREAN WAR, 1950-1953,
AND TO THOSE ENLISTED MEN
WHO WERE IN
THE KOREAN PIPELINE, 1950-1951.

## AUTHOR'S ACKNOWLEDGMENT

"I'm Moving On" was a country music song written by Hank Snow in 1950, and it was No.1 on the Billboard music charts for 21 weeks. The following lyrics come from Hank Snow's song:

THAT BIG EIGHT-WHEELER ROLLIN' DOWN THE TRACK
MEANS YOUR TRUE LOVIN' DADDY AIN'T COMIN' BACK
I'M MOVIN' ON, I'LL SOON BE GONE
YOU WERE FLYIN' TOO HIGH FOR MY LITTLE OLD SKY
I'M MOVING ON.

The Korean War started in 1950, when Hank Snow's song was No.1, and when President Truman ordered the 24th Division into Korea. During the next several months more than 90 percent of the GIs in the 24th Division were killed in action. In their short time in Korea they wrote and sang their own lyrics to Hank Snow's song "I'm Moving On."

The following are some of the lyrics that the men of the 24th Division adapted to Hank Snow's song:

YOU HEAR THE RUMBLE OF RUNNING FEET
THE 24TH DIVISION IS IN FULL RETREAT
WE'RE MOVING ON, WE'RE MOVING ON
CHINESE BUGLES BLOW, WE'VE GOT TO GO
WE'RE MOVING ON.

THE SNOW'S COMING DOWN, IT'S FREEZING TOO
AND NOW WE'RE OFF TO THE BIG YALU
WE'RE MOVING ON, WE'RE MOVING ON
IT'S STARTING TO SNOW, WE'VE GOT TO GO
WE'RE MOVING ON.

MAC ARTHUR SAYS, WE'VE GOT TO ATTACK
BUT YOU FOLLOW MAC AND YOU'LL NEVER COME BACK
WE'RE MOVING ON, WE'RE MOVING ON
YOU FOLLOW MAC AND YOU'LL NEVER COME BACK
WE'RE MOVING ON.

GENERAL RIDGWAY SAYS, YOU CAN'T RETREAT
BUT YOU DON'T RETREAT, YOU'RE GONNA GET BEAT
WE'RE MOVING ON, WE'RE MOVING ON
CHINESE TRUMPETS BLOW, WE'VE GOT TO GO
WE'RE MOVING ON.

THE RAIN'S COMING DOWN, IT'S POURING TOO
WE'VE GOT MUD, UP THE GAZOO
WE'RE MOVING ON, WE'RE MOVING ON
MUD UP TO HERE, HEAD FOR DANGER REAR
WE'RE MOVING ON.

MR. TRUMAN SAYS, IT'S THE DOMINO
FUCK THE DOMINO, IT'S TIME TO GO
WE'RE MOVING ON, WE'RE MOVING ON
CHINESE BURP GUNS BLOW, IT'S TIME TO GO
WE'RE MOVING ON

WE ASKED THE FIRST SERGEANT FOR R and R
AND ALL WE GOT WAS THE BIG HAR! HAR!
WE'RE MOVING ON, WE'RE MOVING ON
ASK FOR R and R, GET THE BIG HAR! HAR!
WE'RE MOVING ON.

GENERAL RIDGWAY SAYS, HAVE NO FEAR
BUT RIDGWAY'S BACK AT DANGER REAR
WE'RE MOVING ON, WE'RE MOVING ON
MATT'S GOT NO FEAR, HE'S IN DANGER REAR
WE'RE MOVING ON.

# PART I
# THE BEGINNING OF THE KOREAN PIPELINE

# *NORTH KOREA INVADES SOUTH KOREA, JUNE 1950*

On June 25, 1950 more than seven divisions of North Korean troops led by T-34 tanks crossed the 38$^{th}$ parallel into South Korea. Six months earlier, the United States Secretary of State, Dean Acheson, in a major foreign policy statement had neglected to include South Korea in the American Asian Defense Perimeter. The only American forces in Korea, at that time, were part of a small advisory mission called the Korean Military Advisory Group (KMAG). The KMAG had been set up in 1946 to assist in the development of the Republic of Korea's armed forces from 1946 through 1950. The resulting South Korean Army was completely unprepared for the North Korean attack, and the Communist invasion was successful and devastating.

All the news from the battlefield in 1950 was negative, and in Washington, President Truman was faced with hard-line Communist haters on one side, and those on the other side who saw the offensive from the North as a Korean civil war. Was this an invasion ordered by Moscow? Were the North Koreans nothing more than pawns in a Russian chess game, and this a first step in their road to world domination? The Domino Theory became a battle cry from right-wing hardliners in the United States Congress as they darkly predicted that Korea would be the first domino to fall, and then Japan, and then we'd be fighting them off in California. President Truman decided to use the United States forces, and in time the United Nations, to draw a line against what he saw as Communist aggression in Korea; aggression that he said challenged the safety of the United States. During the Korean War, which lasted 37 months, the United States ordered more than 5.7 million men into the

Korean theater of war; 34,000 Americans were killed in action; over 20,000 Americans were killed in non-combat accidents; more than 104,000 American soldiers were wounded in action, and over 5,000 were listed as missing in action or as prisoners of war. The South Korean Army suffered 46,000 killed in action and more than 100,000 wounded. The estimates of enemy casualties list Chinese killed in action at 400,000, and the North Koreans suffered 215,000 killed in action.

Military historian S.L.A.Marshall said of Korea that it was the centuries nastiest war. Years after the war was over Dean Acheson said of the Korean conflict, it was a damnable war—politically and militarily. Averell Harriman called it a sour war. For what was once called "a police action" by President Truman, in an effort to sell the war to the American people, more than 700,000 American, Korean and Chinese men were killed in action, and it is still often referred to as "The Forgotten War."

In the summer of 1950, one month after the North Korean tanks crossed the 38th parallel into South Korea, the United States Army mailed out notices to thousands of army inactive reservists, recalling them to active duty. These official notices also informed these reservists that they were being demoted one rank, and gave them a definite time to report for active duty. Many of these men resented this blanket recall, most of whom had already served in combat in World War II, and were now being ordered to serve in combat half-way around the world in what was being called "a police action." These men were ordered to report for active duty within days of their notification; they were then sent to U.S. Army training camps where they went through ten days of combat infantry training (usually at paratrooper army bases); and then herded onto crowded troop trains for a five day trip to the West Coast to replacement depots like Camp Stoneman, California; and then they were loaded onto troop ships, as if they were cattle, and stacked up six or seven deep in the ship's hold on canvas bunks about five feet long. The troop ships' destination was Camp Drake in Yokahama, Japan, another replacement depot. After a short stay at Camp Drake these men were loaded onto another troop train and taken to Sasebo, Japan, and from there they were stacked up on U.S. landing barges and taken to Pusan, Korea. From Pusan the men were again herded onto makeshift troop trains and sent to replacement depots near the front line, and from there sent out to their respective combat units. This journey for these veteran reservists, men between the ages of 20 to 30, lasted about two months, from recall to the front line, and later would become known as the Korean Pipeline.

# PART II
# THE GEOGRAPHY AND CULTURE OF KOREA

## *THE GEOGRAPHY AND CULTURE OF KOREA*

Korea lies adjacent to China and is separated from Japan by the Sea of Japan. The northern border of Korea is formed by the Yalu River and the Tumen River, both of which separate Korea from Manchuria. These rivers would play a prominent role in the Korean War. The west coast of the Korean peninsula is formed by the Korea Bay to the north, and the Yellow Sea to the south, while the east coast of the peninsula is bounded by the Sea of Japan. Because of the geographic location of Korea, close to Japan and China, the cultures from all three societies filtered together combining Buddhism and Confucianism into a common cultural sphere.

The ancient history of the Korean peninsula includes the Mongolian, Turkish and Manchurian tribes that migrated into Korea from China during the Neolithic Age. The first agricultural settlements appeared in the southern part of Korea around 6,000 B.C. In the 17$^{th}$ century, Korea became a vassal state of China and was isolated from the outside world until the Sino-Japanese War of 1894-1895. Japan won the war and established an occupation force in Korea. A large part of Korean history includes the period in the late 1800s when Japan began to force Korea out of China's sphere of influence and into its own. Korea was occupied by Japan for many years, and during the Japanese colonial rule, the Korean language was suppressed in an effort by the Japanese to eradicate Korean national identity. By 1910, Japan had made considerable progress in developing Korea, but had never won over the Korean nationalists, who continued to strive for independence. Koreans were forced to take Japanese surnames, and traditional Korean culture suffered heavy losses, as numerous Korean antiques and artifacts were either destroyed or taken to Japan, where to this day, they may be found in Japanese museums or private collections. There are also many antiques and artifacts from Korea that can be found in the United States.

After Japan surrendered at the conclusion of World War II, the Korean peninsula was partitioned into two occupation zones, separated at the 38th parallel. The Soviet Union controlled the north, and the United States took charge of the south. The division of Korea became permanent in 1948 with the establishment of separate governments of North and South Korea. After the Korean Armistice in 1953, the 38th parallel boundary between North and South Korea became fixed, and became known as the demilitarized zone (DMZ), a four kilometer wide strip of land running along the 38th parallel from east to west for a distance of about 240 kilometers.

Korea compares in size to Great Britain, or about 245,000 square kilometers, and there are about 3,000 islands belonging to Korea. Early in the history of Korea, its land mass included most of Manchuria, but after repeated wars with China, the Koreans finally withdrew southward and the Amnokkong and Tumen Rivers (approximately the line formed by the Yalu River) became the permanent Chinese-Korean border. The major rivers in Korea flow from north to south or from east to west and they empty into the Yellow Sea or the Korea Strait. These rivers, including the Chongchon River in North Korea, figured prominently in the Korean War, and they all tend to be wide and shallow with seasonal variations in water flow.

The Korean winters are usually long, bitterly cold, and dry, and are influenced by the Siberian air mass. The summers are short, hot and humid, and there is a rainy season between June and August which accounts for two thirds of the annual precipitation, and rainfall during this time can be substantial. The weather in the winter, summer and rainy season would figure prominently in the Korean War, and almost always favored the Chinese and North Koreans.

The modern Korean educational system consists of six years in elementary school, three years in middle school, and three years in high school, for a total of twelve years. Most public, middle school and high school students have to wear uniforms, and there are some hygiene regulations, as well. The United Nations school assessment agency, the

Program for International School Assessment, currently ranks South Korea's science education as the 3rd best in the world. The Korean education system, both North and South, are much more strict and structured than most western educational systems. The Korean students rarely have free time outside their school activities and studies, as they are under a lot of parental and societal pressure to perform and gain university entrance.

Although Korea is located at the same latitude as both St. Louis and San Francisco, the mountains and frigid Siberian artic winds from Manchuria, give Korea very cold winters. Regarding the national diet, it is influenced by the weather in both the north and south. A Korean breakfast might consist of a bowl of Tripe soup, or beef soup with lots of rice. The Koreans gather their fish from the Yellow Sea, the Sea of Japan, and the coastal areas to the south where the two seas come together. Seafood is the main feature of the Korean life and diet, and no table is ever without a bowl of dried and salted fish for lunch or dinner, and even for breakfast.

Until modern times, Koreans lived mainly in small farming communities that were concentrated in the arable parts of the peninsula. During those times North Korea was the more industrialized and South Korea was mainly agricultural. Today that has changed, and South Korea has emerged as a strong industrial and economic country.

South Korea
South Korea is about the size of Indiana; it is mountainous in the east toward the Sea of Japan, and in the west and south of the country there are many harbors and off-shore islands.

When the Korean War ended in 1953, South Korea was a devastated country in need of large scale rehabilitation. President Syngman Rhee, the man backed for president by the United States in 1949, was forced to resign in 1960 after twelve years in office, due to rising discontent in the country with his authoritarian leadership. Political instability continued in South Korea through successive political leaders. In June 2000, President Kim Dae Jung of South Korea met with North Korea's president Kim Jong Il in Pyongyang, and it was the first ever meeting of the two countries leaders. National polls have always noted that well over 80 percent of Koreans want a unified Korea, and this presidential meeting was seen as a step in that direction. Then in May 2007, a railroad network was completed between the two countries, and for the first time in 56 years trains passed between North and South Korea. In the future, both Koreas hope that a trans-Korean railroad will provide easier access for Koreans to reach other parts of Asia. In October 2007, President Roh Hyun of South Korea and the North Korean president met for the second inter-Korean summit. The two leaders pledged to work together on several economic projects, and they agreed to move toward signing a treaty that would formally end the Korean War. South Korea was the only party that did not sign the original armistice at Panmunjon in 1953.

North Korea

North Korea is slightly smaller than Pennsylvania, and is almost completely covered by a series of north-south mountain ranges that are separated by narrow valleys. The Yalu River forms part of its northern border with Manchuria and would play an important role in the Korean War.

North Korea has an authoritarian socialist government whose Head of State since 1994 has been Kim Jong Il. The Prime Minister as of 2007 was Kim Yong Il. The Democratic People's Republic of Korea (North Korea) was established in May 1948, with Kim Il Sung as president. After Kim Il Sung's death in 1994, his son, Kim Jong Il became president. During that time there were negotiations with the United Nations over North Korea's suspected possession of nuclear weapons, and an agreement was reached in June 1995 that allowed North Korea to have a nuclear reactor for peaceful purposes and as a supply of energy for the country. North Korea has been accused by the United States of being the world's most secretive society, and the U.S. has also accused them of human rights violations. North Korea has made similar charges against the United States, and accuses the U.S. of wanting to bring about a regime change in North Korea. The North Koreans have argued for a peace treaty with the United States; a treaty that would prohibit the United States from attacking North Korea. This peace treaty has yet to be worked out or signed. Access to North Korea is limited and its country's domestic media is tightly controlled.

In February 2008, the New York Philharmonic played a concert in Pyongyang, the capital of North Korea. It was the first time an American cultural group performed in North Korea and it was the largest American delegation to visit North Korea since the end of the Korean War. The orchestra played pieces by Dvorak, Gershwin, and Wagner. They also played the Star Spangled Banner and a traditional Korean folk song.

Negotiations regarding North Korea's nuclear capability and intentions have continued throughout 2008 and they continue today. The diplomatic roller coaster continued its unpredictable course, and then in October 2008 the United States State Department removed North Korea from its list of state sponsors of terrorism. The situation will remain unstable for some time and even throughout President Barack Obama's term as president.

PART III
NORTH KOREAN INVASION,
KOREAN PIPELINE BEGINS
PUSAN PERIMETER,
INCHON LANDING
RUSH TO THE YALU
JUNE 1950-DECEMBER 1950

# *NORTH KOREAN INVASION, JUNE 25, 1950*

In July 1945 Allied leaders, the President of the United States, Harry Truman; the Premier of Russia, Joseph Stalin; and the Prime Minister of Great Britain, Clement Atlee met in Potsdam, Germany to determine a campaign strategy against Japan in World War II. Four days after the Potsdam Conference the first of two atomic bombs fell on Japan at Hiroshima, and days later a second atomic bomb fell on Nagasaki. On August 14, 1945 Japan surrendered. After Japan's defeat, it became clear to the Americans that there would be competition with the Russians for the possession of the Korean peninsula, which at that time was not part of the United States Asian Defense Perimeter. In August 1945 the Russians and the United States agreed on occupation zones in Korea as a prerequisite for disarming large Japanese garrisons stationed in that country. At that time, Colonel Dean Rusk, then a staff officer in the U.S. Army's Strategy and Planning Branch, entered into an agreement with officers of the Russian Army that the demarcation line should be the 38$^{th}$ parallel of latitude. The 38$^{th}$ parallel runs east-west across the Korean peninsula and virtually passes through the city of Panmunjon, site of the eventual armistice talks. During the next five years the Cold War developed between Russia and the United States and the political scene in Korea became chaotic. The United States set up Syngman Rhee as head of a provisional government in Seoul hoping that he could bring the political forces together in South Korea. However, Syngman Rhee, by then in his seventies, immediately began to complain strongly about the Russians and the Americans, and called for the immediate unification of Korea, and the establishment of a national government with Mr. Rhee as president. It soon became clear to Koreans on both sides of the 38$^{th}$

parallel that their hopes for unification were evaporating, and they watched as Russia and the United States forged ahead with their own plans to separate the country. The arbitrary separation of this nation in 1945 set the stage for what would eventually become a catastrophic war on the Korean peninsula.

The North Korean invasion in June 1950 was preceded by a long and extensive barrage of artillery and mortar fire. This heavy artillery fire was followed by seven infantry divisions of North Korean troops, or approximately 90,000 infantrymen, led by more than 150 T-34 tanks that were backed up by 122 mm howitzers and self-propelled 67 mm guns. The North Koreans also had more than 200 Russian supplied ground attack aircraft that gave them complete air superiority at that time.

What followed in the next several days was a complete rout of the Republic of South Korea(ROK) forces. The Republic of Korea had only four divisions deployed along the 38th parallel, no air force, no recoilless rifles, no heavy mortars, no medium artillery, and no tanks. The North Koreans, led by T-34 tanks which were said to be the best tanks developed during World War II, moved through the South Korean forces as if they weren't there. The ROK infantrymen tried to stop the advance but they only had satchel charges and hand grenades, so they were quickly overcome. The North Koreans attacked in an inverted Y formation, sweeping around the South Koreans, encircling them, and causing many casualties.

In just two days after the start of the invasion, the South Korean capital of Seoul was abandoned, as the North Koreans then moved eastward along the Taebaek Mountains. The North Korean advance was overwhelming and caused chaos among the South Korean forces, and their casualties were high. During the first week of the war, more than a third of the South Korean army, or 34,000 ROKs, were killed in action, taken prisoner, or reported missing.

The Republic of Korea forces fought bravely and inflicted heavy losses on the North Korean army, but they were not able to slow them down or stop their advance. The North Koreans are reported to have been well trained, and a third of them had fought in the Chinese civil war. During the first weeks of the war, the North Koreans wiped out five

ROK divisions, and it is reported that if they had not paused to regroup in July 1950, but had continued their assault toward the south, they probably would have captured Pusan and all of South Korea before the United States, and eventually the United Nations, had time to build up their forces and stage a successful counterattack. However, the United States entered the war, and in July 1950, the 24th Division was deployed to Korea to slow down or stop the North Korean advance. This infusion of American troops into the battle caused the North Koreans to pause, and allowed the United States time to reinforce their troop strength. However, the 24th Division suffered heavy losses before they were relieved by the First Cavalry, as their Division went from 16,000 men on July 1, to 9,000 men on July 22. And in the weeks and months to come in Korea, the battlefield situation would not improve for the Americans.

After the initial attack in June 1950, the North Koreans captured Seoul on June 27. Then by July 4 they had taken over the airstrip at Suwon, just south of Seoul. Following the battle at Suwon, the North Koreans advanced to Osan where they encountered and defeated the American 24th Division, Task Force Smith, who then had to withdraw south to Taejon. By July 14, the 34th Regiment of the 24th Division was overrun at Chonan. Finally, by July 16 the American and ROK defensive lines at the Kum River were broken down, and then on August 4 the North Koreans crossed the Pusan Perimeter at the Naktong River.

## THE KOREAN PIPELINE, AUGUST 1950

Michael Parker received his U.S. Army recall notification in August 1950. Parker had served in World War II and was discharged in 1947. After his discharge he entered college on the G.I. Bill and was in his third year at college when his recall notice arrived. The Korean War, only months underway in 1950, took place before television news came into prominence. In those days, television news shows were short and of marginal influence on the public, and the footage from Korea that made it to the television screen was often shown several days after the events took place, and rarely had an effect on the nation as a whole. Michael Parker, at that time, had no idea about the politics regarding the country's decision to enter Korea with U.S. ground forces, so his reaction to receiving his recall to active duty was initially disbelief, and then followed by anger and resentment.

Parker and his date, Anne, were sitting in a bar in Upstate New York talking about the recall of reservists.

"Can we do anything to get you out of this recall?," Anne said.

"The only thing we can do is check with the college ROTC officer about a deferment. And also, if we know somebody with influence, we can ask them to contact the local U.S. Army reserve office to see what options we might have. It doesn't look good. I don't know anyone who has gotten out of this recall."

One week after this conversation, Michael Parker reported to Camp Campbell, Kentucky and was assigned to a military barracks, issued military fatigues, combat boots, and an M-1 rifle. He was told that he would be taking a ten day course in combat infantry training. He was also told that after the ten days of basic training he would be sent to a West Coast army base to await further orders.

The ten day courses in combat training given to all reservists were conducted by instructors at army paratrooper bases in the United States. However, these courses did not turn out the way the paratrooper instructors wanted them to. Every morning the company was called out in formation at 5:30 am, and every morning, more than 75 percent of the company left the formation and reported for sick call. It should be noted, that all of these men had served in World War II, many of them in combat, and they wanted no part of this Korean War. And these veteran reservists thought these young paratroopers were nothing but gung-ho ass-holes. The closest these paratroopers had been to combat was the infiltration course they went through during basic training, or the transition firing range where they fired off rounds with their M-1 or carbine. After a few days of the whole company reporting for sick call, a young 2nd lieutenant company commander called for a formation of all company personnel. The entire company was front and center at 5:30 in the morning; no one was allowed to go on sick call until the 2nd lieutenant had addressed them.

"You men have been recalled to active duty to defend the freedom of our country," the 2nd lieutenant started out. "You WILL be here for two weeks, and during that time you WILL report to duty every day. You WILL NOT, I repeat WILL NOT avoid reporting for duty by going on sick call. If you do go on sick call you'd better be sick. Those of you who report for sick call, and are found to be faking it, WILL then be sent to the mess hall to pull KP duty every day until the company completes their training." The 2nd lieutenant stood there, staring at the men in front of him, trying to look tough—then he did a facing movement and marched off to the orderly room. The next morning the company was called out at 5:30 am, and at 5:35 am more than 80 percent of the company reported for sick call. That's the way it went for the next two weeks, with the paratrooper instructors giving "training" classes to about 20 percent of the company. One part of the training included a day at the rifle range, usually a transition range with distances to the target of 100 to 300 yards. The reservists on the firing line, however, were not interested in achieving a top score on the range. They knew that a good score on the transition range would go on their service record, and increase their chances of being sent to the front line. Most of the men were firing their weapons at anything downrange except their own target. When no one qualified at the rifle range, the company commander held another company formation, and threatened the reservists again.

Standing in front of the company of men he had been put in charge of, a group of men that were not listening to him, the 2$^{nd}$ lieutenant said, "You WILL complete this exercise, and you WILL qualify on this range. Anyone who does not qualify, WILL be subject to strict disciplinary action." With that the 2$^{nd}$ lieutenant company commander saluted his 1$^{st}$ sergeant, did another facing movement and headed for the orderly room.

This 21 tear old company commander, making all these "You Will" statements to this company of veterans, was 14 years old when Michael Parker, in 1943 and in his last year of high school, walked out of a John Wayne war movie and went directly to a U.S. Army recruiting office and signed up for active duty with the army. Parker went on to serve in combat in Europe and was discharged in 1947. He never felt comfortable with all the military protocol in the army and when his time was up he was more than ready to leave active duty. His big mistake at that time, as it turned out, was to agree to sign up in the inactive reserves. Yet after his recall in 1950, Michael Parker realized right away that he was headed for Korea, so he completed the ten day course in combat training with the intention of honing his combat skills. He did not report to sick call as did many others in his company. He felt that he had to get ready for Korea for his own survival, so he learned all that he could; he got acquainted once again with the M-1 rifle—how to take it apart, clean it, and put it back together; he fired all the weapons including the BAR, mortars, and the recoilless rifle; and he practiced bayonet drills and trench warfare. After completing the course at Camp Campbell, Michael Parker joined the rest of his division and boarded the overcrowded troop train that would take him on a five day trip to Camp Stoneman, California, an army replacement depot in California that was set up to transport troops to Japan, and then on to Korea.

Parker got a two day pass after completing his combat course, so before leaving Kentucky for the West Coast he flew Anne to the town outside the army base, and they spent two days in a motel right outside the gate. They had the feeling that they might not see each other again, they had a sense of urgency. They made love for 48 hours, almost non-stop, and then, before boarding the troop train they went downtown and Michael bought Anne an engagement ring.

It was August 1950, barely two months after the North Koreans invaded South Korea, when Michael Parker boarded the troop train headed for the West Coast and from there to await orders for Korea.

\* \* \* \* \*

James Foley was attending college as a pre-med student at the University of Maryland in July 1950 when he received his army recall notification. He had served in the occupation of the 2$^{nd}$ World War. After graduation from high school in 1945 he enlisted in the U.S. Army and was stationed in Italy where he was assigned to a military police battalion. He completed his military police basic training in Pisa, Italy before being stationed in Florence. The military duty during the occupation was considered good duty, that is, compared to active combat. However, the military police had a reputation for being a rigorous outfit with strict discipline and difficult guard duty schedules. As an enlisted man, James Foley was assigned to eight hour guard shifts at locations such as officers' hotels, generals' trailers, and other buildings that had been taken over by the U.S. Army. Another assignment given to the military police was traffic duty. The MP was set up in the middle of a traffic intersection and for an eight hour shift was required to direct traffic, while always standing at attention; arms always held out in a stiff military manner, and all movements had to be facing movements. The MP on duty was also required to salute all officers and all staff cars, regardless if any officers were riding inside those staff cars; and any MP who missed a salute was subject to disciplinary action. Duty as a military policeman was not easy duty, but certainly better than similar duty under wartime conditions.

After receiving his recall notice, James Foley talked with several influential business and professional acquaintances, including a congressman, regarding his options and a possible deferment from this army recall. A deferment on the grounds of attending college was tried; a national guard deferment was investigated; but none of these possibilities were successful. Once in the Korean Pipeline, it was turning out to be impossible to get out of it. At the end of July 1950, James Foley reported to a paratrooper army camp in North Carolina to begin a ten day course in combat infantry training. He was told that upon completion of this training course he would be transferred by troop train to an army replacement depot on the West Coast, to await assignment to Korea.

* * * * *

David Hansen was a freshman law student at the University of Miami in Coral Gables, Florida in July 1950 when he received his reserve recall to active military duty. Hansen, it turned out, was not surprised when his recall notice showed up in the mail. He was a law student, but he was also a political junkie, and he was up-to-date on all domestic and international events. He had read about Korea and about the North Korean invasion across the 38th parallel into South Korea. He knew that President Truman had committed U.S. forces to Korea, and that he was seeking United Nations support to turn back the North Koreans. He also had read that Truman planned to recall all reservists to active duty. However, it was still a shock to actually receive the army recall notice. He saw everything he had planned and worked for, heading down the tubes, for at least two years and maybe more. And who knew what might happen once you got to Korea. He had read all the negative battle news from the war zone; you might even end up in a Korean rice paddy. Hansen tried to get an educational deferment; he tried to join the National Guard; he wrote his congressman; all to no avail. It would soon become evident to everyone involved, that once in the Korean Pipeline, you didn't get out until you arrived in Korea.

On August 1, 1950, two months after the North Koreans entered South Korea, David Hansen reported for active duty to Camp

Campbell, Kentucky. His military occupation service number (MOS) was changed from Special Service NCO to infantry rifleman, and he was told to report to Baker Company, 82$^{nd}$ Airborne, to begin a ten day refresher course in combat training in preparation for transfer to the Korean theater of war.

## *TASK FORCE SMITH, JULY 1950*

The first American infantry soldiers arrived in Korea in July 1950. They were part of the 24th Infantry Division. Their commanding officer, Lt. Colonel Smith, was given only 24 hours notice to leave their base in Japan and be flown to an airfield as close as possible to the front line. These men were from the 21st Infantry Regiment and their expedition became known as Task Force Smith. There were about 400 of them, and they were taken by train and road to Pyongtaek, a town on the Seoul-Pusan highway.

Shortly after dawn on July 5, the men of Task Force Smith faced the enemy for the first time. A column of North Korean T-34 tanks came down on them from Suwan, a town about 20 miles north of Pyongtaek. The T-34 tanks drove straight through their defensive positions, while enemy mortar fire plastered the American soldiers; and the enemy infantry swarmed from around their tanks and spread throughout the disorganized and unprepared American soldiers of Task Force Smith, killing them at random. Colonel Smith gave the order to retreat and the survivors began to stagger back toward the rear, across rice paddies reeking from human and animal manure.

That night, what was left of Task Force Smith reached Ansong, a village near their base camp at Pyongtaek. The officer in charge at Ansong was the senior artillery officer for the 24th Division Artillery, and he ordered the men to hold their ground. It was raining very hard and the men sat around miserably, out in the open, not wanting to get into their water filled foxholes. In the meantime, the North Korean tanks moved forward maintaining constant firepower on the Americans. The American unit was in almost complete paralysis. None of these men had really expected to see combat, and they had even been told by their officers that now that the Americans had entered the war, the North Koreans would surrender, lay down their arms and retreat.

These men had spent the last four years as part of an occupying force in Japan and had no combat training or experience. They had spent their time living on the Japanese economy, drinking Japanese beer and whiskey, and enjoying their women. They were completely unprepared, militarily and psychologically, for the dangerous and potentially disastrous situation they were thrown into. These men of the 24th Division were nothing more than cannon fodder, they were expendable as far as the military high-level officers were concerned, and they were thrown in front of a large advancing army of tanks and infantry to slow down their advance, giving time for the U.S. Army to send in more experienced replacements. As the advancing North Korean tanks gave covering fire to their infantry, the enemy quickly moved among the Americans causing terrible casualties, and the collapse of Task Force Smith. Those who survived the initial attack were soon moving rapidly to the rear, some without their packs which were too heavy to allow free movement, and many without their weapons.

The remnants of Task Force Smith finally reached Chonan, a village about 20 miles south of Pyongtaek where they were ordered to set up a defensive perimeter. This order was met with outbursts of swearing and grumbling, and many of the men refused to obey the order as they continued to withdraw toward the rear. The men who stayed had nothing to use to "dig in" their position, as most of them had thrown away their entrenching tools. The only food the men could get, they had to take from Korean farmers. And during this time, rumors were flying everywhere; a train was waiting down the line to take them back to Pusan; their reinforcements were already on the way; soon they would all be back in Japan. However, the reality was that the North Korean tanks kept coming and the enemy infantry was swarming all over their positions. The damage to Task Force Smith was devastating and almost complete—when someone finally shouted, " Let's get the hell out of here." What was left of the 24th Division was soon in full retreat.

# GENERAL MACARTHUR'S RESPONSE TO THE NORTH KOREAN ATTACK

When the North Koreans attacked, General Douglas MacArthur was slow to respond and seemed indifferent to the news of the invasion. There were early reports that MacArthur could not believe that the North Koreans would so blatantly challenge the United States military under his command. He is reported to have said, " If only Washington and Truman will not hobble me, I can handle this with one arm behind my back." MacArthur, once a jaunty, confident military figure, was now in his seventies, and he seemed to be transformed overnight into a dejected, forlorn man as the news from Korea worsened. MacArthur had wanted no part of Korea from 1945 to 1950. The only time he visited Korea during that time was for the inauguration of Syngman Rhee as the South Korean president. If MacArthur had little interest in Korea, this attitude was typical of American political opinion at that time. Korea was definitely not connected to the American political process or the American psychological make-up. However, as the Cold War intensified, the relationship between the United States and Korea became one of interest and concern. The threat of global Communism, as seen by many hard-liners in the United States government, pushed Korea into the forefront of political discourse in America.

The Domino Theory, as promoted by right leaning members of the United States Congress, became a battle cry. "Fight them over there—not in California"; "Protect our freedom: Fight in Korea—not in the United States." These slogans spread throughout the country and were soon taken as fact by the majority of people in the United States, just as they are today as the country is warned that we must "fight the terrorists

## THE KOREAN PIPELINE

over there(as in Iraq), not over here." So when North Korea crossed the 38th parallel in June 1950, Korea became a country for which President Truman and the United States government determined that Americans should be willing to fight and die for.

General MacArthur's slow response to action on the ground in Korea, recalled to some, his lack of preparation before the start of the war with Japan in World War II. At that time he completely underestimated the strength of Japanese forces and their ability to strike American possessions in the Pacific. Because of this lack of preparation, his command had allowed Japanese bombers to destroy American aircraft under his command at Wake Island, as they sat on the ground for nine hours after the attack on Pearl Harbor. British historian Max Hastings wrote that MacArthur was responsible for the U.S. military debacle in the Philippines in 1941-1942, yet he escaped any share of the blame for it. The rules that applied to other officers and men never seemed to apply to Douglas MacArthur. When the Korean War began, however, MacArthur, although in his seventies, was described by his staff as a man of vigor and energy. Yet among those who were not part of his inner circle, there were ominous signs about his health and age related conditions. General Joseph Stilwell, who watched MacArthur accept the Japanese surrender in 1945, noted how badly his hands were shaking as he signed documents. Stilwell chalked it off to the pressures surrounding the occasion, but General Walter Krueger, who was one of MacArthur's senior officers, told Stilwell that it was Parkinson's Disease.

In MacArthur's distinguished career, there were many ups and downs. There were times when he was far less the brilliant commander, and more the vainglorious individual, and as a consequence others, such as the troops under his command, would pay the price for these failures. However, in 1950, General Douglas MacArthur was still a formidable figure. He had been a famous and daring commander in World War I, had conducted a shrewd and tactical campaign against the Japanese in the Pacific, and at the outbreak of the Korean War he was credited for having done an excellent job of aiding Japan in post World War II.

In the first months of the Korean War, Major General William Dean was commander of the 24th Division. If he hoped that the defeats at

Pyongtaek and Chonan were the worst of his campaign, then he would be proven wrong. The town of Taejon, farther south on the road to Pusan, was General Dean's divisional headquarters which held supplies, weapons, ammunition, fuel and rations. The North Korean advance headed south toward General Dean's headquarters after wiping out Task Force Smith. It is reported that General Dean, at that time, was leading a bazooka company that was on foot attempting to stop the T-34 tanks from advancing on his headquarters. However, the North Korean tanks went smashing through Taejon, spraying the buildings, homes and American soldiers with machine gun fire. According to reports, General Dean attempted to stop the enemy advance with his anti-tank squad but the North Koreans closed in on all sides. The 24th Division was again not prepared for this magnitude of assault, and the Division was routed again in Taejon, as had happened in Pyongtaek. The Americans, unable to hold off the enemy advance, began heading south, leaving their weapons, equipment and trucks behind them. General Dean is also reported to have retreated on foot, and he apparently wandered around for nearly a month, in the hills surrounding Taejon, before being captured. He was released from captivity when the armistice was reached in 1953 and was awarded the Congressional Medal of Honor.

In the months that followed these field disasters, there would be substantial changes in the American Army in Korea, and they would finally be able to gain the initiative. However, in the early months of the war, the battles were being directed by officers who sat back at Danger Rear, who only occasionally visited their enlisted men on the front lines. Radio communication, voice and Morse code, was erratic, and radio operators were a prime target of the enemy. It was, therefore, impossible for the officers to maintain communication and control of their units while they stayed back at the Command Post. "Bug Out Fever" was systemic among the troops, and both American and Republic of Korea enlisted men were heading south, and the retreat was not an organized one. The Americans were out-manned and out-gunned and had only their survival instincts to rely on. There was only the hope that they would be able to regroup later and then attempt to take the initiative.

## THE KOREAN PIPELINE

As American and ROK forces were retreating during the initial weeks of the war, the United States government submitted a United Nation's resolution, asking member nations to offer ships and troops to assist the United States forces. This July 1950 resolution had an initial disappointing response; yet given the disastrous situation on the ground in Korea at that time, and following the defeat of Colonel Smith's Task Force, this United Nation's response should have been expected. Regardless, it was not long before several nations began sending reinforcements to Korea; however the situation in the war zone still remained critical.

On the positive side, within weeks of the start of the war, the North Korean Air Force had been defeated by the United States Air Force. And at sea, maritime supremacy was achieved and a tight blockade was established around the entire Korean peninsula. These conditions in the air and at sea, although favorable and still outweighed by the extensive losses on the ground, gave General MacArthur the confidence he needed to begin thinking in terms of an amphibious landing to the rear of the enemy. This attack took place at Inchon harbor in September 1950 and was successful. It has been acknowledged to have been a turning point in the Korean War, and one of General MacArthur's most successful campaign achievements. There are many military analysts, however, who now believe that the success of the Inchon landing, also succeeded in clouding MacArthur's judgment in the months following Inchon, as he ordered American troops across the 38$^{th}$ parallel and north toward Manchuria.

## PUSAN PERIMETER, JULY-SEPTEMBER 1950

In late July and into August 1950, the North Korean infantry and armored divisions, were heading south toward Pusan. The roads were jammed with convoys of American trucks and soldiers trying to move toward the rear and relative safety, and the fighting from Taejon south toward Pusan resulted in a rout for American and Republic of Korea forces. Most of the replacements were right out of civilian life, untrained and demoralized after a few days in Korea. And the regular army men were former clerks, orderlies, supply and quartermaster NCOs, and mechanics—and the reality on the ground in Korea came as a dreadful shock to them.

However, as the American war machine recovered from the initial surprise and shock of the North Korean invasion, the Pentagon ordered four more divisions into Korea immediately. This was followed by more naval and air reinforcements. By the end of the first week in August the situation on the ground had stabilized to some degree. General Walton Walker was sent to Korea by General MacArthur to command the United States and United Nations ground forces known as the 8th Army. On August 1,1950, General Walker ordered a withdrawal of all United Nations ground forces to a location east of the Naktong River. The General's plan for the 8th Army was to establish a defensive line beyond which American and United Nations forces would not withdraw, and thereby give the United States Army the time it needed to build up its forces and launch a counter offensive. The Pusan Perimeter enclosed a rectangular area of about 100 miles from north to south, and 50 miles east to west. The western boundary of the perimeter was formed by the Naktong River. The eastern and southern boundaries were formed by the

# THE KOREAN PIPELINE

Sea of Japan and the Korea Strait. The northern boundary was an irregular line that ran westward through mountain ranges from Waegwan to Yongdok, and then turned south when it reached the Naktong River, just north of Taegu.

The North Koreans had four attack points, that if taken, would lead them to Pusan. During the first week in August, the North Koreans attacked all of these locations simultaneously. These approaches included, first: an attack through Masan in the south where the Nam River joins the Naktong River; second: through the Naktong River bulge leading to the large rail and road terminals; third: through the city of Taegu; and fourth: through Kyongju, a city on the east coast that would open a corridor toward Pusan.

During the first week of August, General Walker launched an 8th Army counterattack along the Chinju Masan corridor, an area west of Pusan along the coast. The American attack was called Task Force Dean, named for the 24th Division commander, and the Task Force consisted of the 25th Infantry Regiment, a field artillery battalion with the 5th RCT attached. The plan of attack was to move west from Masan, seize the Chinju Pass, and secure a position along the Nam River. Task Force Dean launched its attack on August 7 but immediately ran into a North Korean strike force that was attempting to advance eastward toward Pusan. After several days of heavy fighting neither side could claim victory; however, by launching the Task Force Dean counterattack, the American 8th Army had successfully halted a North Korean assault that, if it had been successful, would have led directly to Pusan.

Seven miles north of where the Naktong River turns east and is joined by the Nam River, is an area that became known as the Naktong Bulge. On August 6, as part of the coordinated North Korean attack on Pusan, the North Korean 4th Division crossed the Naktong River in the Bulge area intent on driving to Pusan. The North Koreans carried no heavy weapons or mortars that would slow their advance, so after crossing the Naktong River they were able to move quickly toward the American lines. Their objective was to capture the town of Yongsan, located about eight miles behind the lines of the United States 24th Infantry Division. This North Korean advance toward U.S. defensive lines became known as the Battle of the Naktong Bulge, a key part of the North Korean offensive plan against the American and South Korean armies defending the Pusan Perimeter. This battle in defense of the Pusan Perimeter would prove to be one of the bloodiest battles of the Korean War.

The Naktong Bulge is located where the Naktong River joins the Nam River, and at this point the Naktong curves westward in a wide semi-circular loop that forms what American troops called the Naktong Bulge. By August 7, the North Koreans had established bridgeheads and secured terrain that allowed them to see all the way to their objective city of Yongsan, five miles to the east. The Americans knew that if the North Koreans were allowed to succeed at the Battle of the Naktong Bulge, they would have a clear corridor all the way to Pusan. This time the North Koreans met the American 24th Division who was defending this sector of the Pusan Perimeter. Also defending this sector were the infantry regiments of the 2nd Division, 25th Division, and the 1st Marine Brigade.

Major General John Church, who replaced Major General William Dean after Dean was captured by the North Koreans, created Task Force Hill whose purpose was to drive the enemy back across the Naktong River. However, the North Koreans counterattacked and Task Force Hill failed in its mission, and they took heavy casualties. General Church, however, continued to attack, and along with artillery and air support the Americans held their defensive positions and caused the enemy to retreat. The fighting lasted throughout the month of August 1950 with heavy casualties on both sides, and then reached a stalemate in early September 1950. The American forces had prevailed and decisively held off the North Korean 4th Division, a Division that reportedly lost half of its original strength in the fighting. The United States 2nd Infantry Division, the 24th Infantry Division and the Marines had held their ground at the Battle of the Naktong Bulge, and then in September 1950, following the successful U.S. amphibious landing at Inchon, the Americans pushed the North Koreans back across the Naktong River, and then forced them to retreat from the Pusan Perimeter and withdraw deep into North Korean territory.

A third front of the North Korean attack on the Pusan Perimeter was located on the east coast at the port city of Pohang-dong . The capture of this port city would also open a corridor for the North Korean Peoples Army to move directly south along the coast to Pusan. In early August, the North Koreans sent three divisions into battle against the Republic of Korea (South Korean) forces. By August 12, the North Koreans had moved toward Pohang-dong and threatened to take a near-by airfield. General Walker sent American reinforcements to support the South Korean forces, and by August 17 the Americans and South Koreans had managed to stop the enemy drive at Pohang-dong. One of the main reasons for the American and South Korean success was that the North Korean supply lines were long and mountainous, and United States airpower was able to be successfully employed, causing heavy casualties to enemy troops.

A fourth axis of attack by the North Koreans occurred during the second week of August. This area included the natural corridor of the Naktong River Valley stretching from Sangju and going southeast to Taegu, the current provisional South Korean capital. The North Koreans had massed sizable forces in an arc around Taegu during the second week in August that included five infantry divisions and an armored division. The American forces included the 1st Cavalry Division and two Republic of Korea infantry divisions. The enemy began a heavy artillery barrage on Taegu on August 18, and that prompted South Korean President Syngman Rhee to move the provisional government from Taegu to Pusan.

On August 19 the North Koreans crossed the Naktong River and advanced toward Taegu using land routes from the north and northwest. At that time, General Walker, Commander of the 8th Army, moved the 23rd and 27th Infantry Divisions into the Taegu area to reinforce the Republic of Korea infantry. The combined defense and counter attack by the Americans and South Koreans were able to effectively stop the enemy efforts to move into Taegu. Allied air strikes, dropping bombs and napalm, were also instrumental in halting the North Korean assault on Taegu.

The American and South Korean defenders of the Pusan Perimeter in early August 1950, successfully resisted the enemy attacks on all four fronts, thereby allowing much needed time for the Allies to build up their forces for a counter offensive. By mid August, General Walker's 8th Army was holding the Pusan Perimeter with what was left of the Republic of Korea army and four depleted American infantry divisions. There was a total of 65,000 men holding back the North Koreans along the Pusan Perimeter. The Republic of Korea forces held the eastern front by the Sea of Japan, and the American forces were placed westward toward the city of Taegu, where they could support the front line at its most vulnerable points. General Walker now had tanks at his disposal, and his force was able to slow down and stop the enemy advance by moving his tanks and troops across the front line as new threats developed.

The Pusan Perimeter became a "hold at all cost" battlefield situation, and the combined efforts of the American and South Korean forces, supplemented by United States air superiority, ended in a successful defense of the Pusan Perimeter. The battles were intense with heavy casualties on both sides. It is reported that the Americans that had been killed in action by mid-September were more than 5,000 battle deaths (400 to 500 per week), 12,000 wounded, and more than 2,000 missing in action or captured.

After the successful defense of the Pusan Perimeter, the American and United Nations forces were able to regroup and stage a strong counterattack, breakout from the Pusan Perimeter, and head north. The breakout from Pusan, along with the successful landing at Inchon by the 1st Marine Division and the 8th Army's 7th Infantry Division, forced a withdrawal of North Korean troops northward past the 38th parallel and back into North Korea.

# *TROOP REINFORCEMENT CAMPAIGN*

The United States started a huge manpower reinforcement campaign to support the troops in Korea in 1950. There was also a massive expansion of the Military Sea Transport Service (MSTS). This involved the decommissioning of hundreds of transport ships, assault ships, and troop ships that had been in moth balls since 1945. This Military Sea Transport Service became part of the Korean Pipeline as it brought supplies, weapons, tanks, and troops across the Pacific and into Korea on a large scale, and supported the United States and United Nations effort for the rest of the war.

In early September 1950, the North Koreans attacked along the Naktong River, from Pohang, an eastern port city on the Sea of Japan, westward to Taegu. As the Communists advanced south from Pohang they got to within four miles of the ancient city of Kyongju before General Walker rushed his 8th Army troops to that front in order to support his Republic of Korea allies. The Americans counter-attacked and the enemy held back.

According to reports, the North Korean Peoples Army sustained over 10,000 casualties during September 1950, and their over-stretched lines of communication and supply were under constant attack by the United States Air Force. The Air Force had just emerged as a separate service in 1947, having previously been the United States Army Air Corps, and as a new service it was attempting to assert its own strength and identity. The U.S.A.F. was led by Generals Vandenberg and Stratemeyer. It was another Air Force general, however, who was getting the headlines in those days, by making bellicose and racist statements about the North Koreans. "We should bomb those Gooks back into the Stone Age," he is reported to have said. In fact, the U.S.A.F. did bomb Korea methodically during the next two years, essentially leveling the country. The use of ordnance, napalm and DDT was indiscriminate during this bombing campaign and the Korean population was literally driven underground. However, according to military reports, the North Korean population remained determined and resolute until the armistice was signed in 1953.

General MacArthur's assessment in July 1950 that four more divisions were needed immediately in Korea was not the news that President Truman wanted to hear. Within a week of MacArthur's troop request, Truman sent a presidential mission, led by Averell Harriman, to MacArthur's headquarters in Tokyo, to meet with him and his staff, and then report back to the president. MacArthur took this opportunity to make a lengthy presentation to convince his presidential guests of his need for massive troop reinforcement. He also took the opportunity to outline his heretofore undisclosed plan to make an amphibious landing at Inchon, a location behind the current enemy front line. MacArthur's presentation apparently mesmerized Averell Harriman and his presidential mission members, for on their return to the United States it is reported that they endorsed all of MacArthur's demands. Harriman reportedly recommended to President Truman that "political and personal consideration should be put to one side, and our government should deal with General MacArthur on the lofty level of the great national asset that he is." It seems that the Harriman delegation did not detect the initial signs of the megalomania that would shortly take over MacArthur. They also apparently overlooked MacArthur's bellicose statements about protecting Formosa from Communist China, and threatening to fly there and assume command, to deliver a crushing defeat to the Chinese, and turn back Communism.

President Truman, along with the Joint Chiefs of Staff, were becoming more and more critical of MacArthur and did not trust his judgment. Truman not only disagreed with MacArthur, but he was also concerned that his commander in Tokyo was taking policy into his own hands. The president also feared that to turn MacArthur loose could lead to a possible war with Communist China, and that the resulting conflict and casualties would be disastrous, with no rational goal in sight.

On September 1, 1950, President Truman addressed the nation to outline his Korean policy, and to put his own views directly before the American people. He described the North Korean aggression, outlined the American response, stated that he did not want the conflict to escalate into all out war, and finally, he did not want the Chinese to be misled by MacArthur's bellicose statements, into possibly entering the war on the side of the North Koreans. Truman went on to say the United States does not believe in aggression or preventive war, and the American soldiers are fighting today for peace in Korea. President Truman's conflict with General Douglas MacArthur came to a head in 1951, when he fired MacArthur and replaced him with General Matthew Ridgway.

# TROOP MOVEMENT IN THE KOREAN PIPELINE

The troop trains that took Corporal Hansen, Sergeant Foley and Tech Sergeant Parker to the West Coast were all part of the massive reinforcement campaign that funneled fighting men, mostly reservists during the first weeks and months of the war, into the Korean War zone. These trains were taken over by the United States government and converted into makeshift troop carriers. After completing their combat training these men were ordered onto these overcrowded trains, that for the next four to five days were home for these troops. The men stood in line all day; in line for three meals a day; in line for cigarettes; in line for rations and supplies; and in line for the latrine. The latrine consisted of a hole in the floor at one end of the rail car, with a handle bar on the wall to hold on to, and the men were lucky if these latrines were walled off for privacy. All of these men knew they were headed for Korea, and none of them wanted to go there. Their morale could not get any lower, and most of them felt that no matter what happened or what they did, they had nothing to lose. Every time the train stopped at a railroad crossing, a town, or at a military base to pick up more troops, there were always some who took the opportunity to jump off the train and head for home. At that time any future consequences didn't bother them. Later, however, when they got home and had time to think about their circumstances, many of them began to reconsider. They had been in the army before and knew that they were absent without official leave (AWOL), and AWOL during time of war was a serious offense. Many of them reported back for duty before being apprehended by the military police, but many held out and were brought back under guard. None of these men faced military

## THE KOREAN PIPELINE

disciplinary action after returning to duty. They were simply restricted to their barracks, and then put back into the pipeline that would take them eventually to Korea.

The troop trains brought these men to points of embarkation on the West Coast, and one of those was Camp Stoneman, California, located about one hour north of San Francisco. Camp Stoneman was set up to process thousands of men as they passed through the army base, their stay lasting about a week. This was the last chance these men would have to contact their loved ones or relatives; their last chance to spend time in the United States before shipping out; and it was their last chance to get a leave. Many of them went home for two or three days, and many others went to San Francisco where they drank, stayed drunk everyday while they were there, or stayed with prostitutes until their leave was up. Eventually, most of them reported back to duty; the ones that did not report back were ready to face the consequences.

Michael Parker, James Foley, and David Hansen all went through Camp Stoneman. Parker obtained leave and went home for a few days with his fiance; James Foley arranged for his wife to fly to San Francisco where they spent a few days together; and David Hansen spent three days in Oakland, drinking and paying for women to keep him company in his hotel room. They all reported back to Camp Stoneman when their leave was up, and then got ready to embark on a troop ship for the crossing of the Pacific Ocean and on to Yokahama, Japan.

On September 1, 1950, less than two months after the North Korean invasion, thousands of soldiers were loaded onto army semis and driven to a staging area near San Francisco. The men had on their fatigues, combat boots, helmets, a 50 pound duffle bag and an M-1 rifle; and they were all held in formation in the staging area while they waited to board the troop ship. They stood in formation, answered roll call with their last name and last four numbers of their army serial number, stood in formation some more, listened to the men griping and calling out, "Hurry up and wait." Finally the commanding officer gave the order to move out and the men started marching off in formation toward the waiting troop ship. At that time the army band had arrived and started playing "Sentimental Journey" as the men staggered off toward the gang plank of the troop ship. The selection of "Sentimental Journey" as a marching song for troops going off to a war zone, was incredible. The officer in charge of the band should have been reassigned to the infantry and sent to Korea on the next troop ship.

Troop ships that were used to transport enlisted men during the first year of the Korean War were called "Victory ships," which were merchant marine vessels used during World War II, and then taken out of moth balls and used for the Korean War. The soldiers heading overseas were marched onto the troop ships and then down into their respective holds. Their bunks, five and one half feet long canvas racks, were stacked up six to eight deep and jammed into these holds with no room to spare. The men had to share their bunks with their 50 pound duffle bag and M-1 rifle; they didn't have room to turn over. The conditions in these holds for enlisted men were not only appalling and dismal, they were extreme health hazards. There was no circulated air, no ventilation system, the air was fetid and filled with bacteria and live viruses, and the area never got cleaned properly. As soon as these troop ships left the dock and got out into the open ocean and started rolling in the waves, many of these GIs got seasick, and some were so sick they never got out of their bunks for the whole month it took for the ship to get from California to Japan. The only exercise these men got was when they rolled over in their bunks and threw up on the deck below. If they happened to be on the top bunk, then the men below them got sprayed with what they threw up. Some of these men never made it to Japan as they died en route of malnutrition, dehydration and diarrhea while down in the hold. Many of the ones who were seasick and survived the ordeal across the Pacific, had to be carrried off the ship when it docked in Japan, and taken to an army hospital in Yokahama, all of them suffering from dehydration and diarrhea. The only thing that can be said for those who didn't survive the 30 days on the troop ship, is that they had been headed for the front line in Korea anyway, and probably would have ended up on the wrong side of a fixed bayonet or a Chinese burp gun, and left to sink into a manure filled Korean rice paddy.

The latrines on these troop ships were never meant to accommodate the large number of GIs jammed on board, so that even on good days when the latrines were functioning normally, these areas were pathetic. However, there never were any good days for enlisted men on these troop ships, and the johns were always overflowing with feces and urine spreading all over the floors. The whole place smelled like an unventilated hog farm, and the potential for disease was always present. Another aspect of these enlisted men's latrines on the troop ship was the shower area. There is nothing like a large group of naked GIs standing around in a small shower, with only cold salt water coming out of the shower head, if the shower was working at all. There was never any soap, and even if there was soap, you couldn't work up a lather in the cold salt water.

The mess halls for enlisted men on these ships would not pass even a basic health department inspection. The food served up was greasy, often undercooked, and thrown onto grimy metal army trays, as the soldiers passed through the chow line. Very often the men had to eat standing up, so that a larger number of them could be run through the mess hall faster, and as they ate standing up, they had to hang onto their trays to keep them from sliding back and forth on the counter in front of them, as the ship rolled sharply in the ocean waves. Due to the lack of hygiene on board, the inability to properly clean the metal army food trays, and the uncooked greasy food, many of the men developed dysentery and other food borne diseases from which many of them did not survive. There were no medical facilities on board, and the only medicines available were the famous army APCs, an aspirin product; "take two APCs, and get back on deck" were the encouraging words from the army medics handing out the pills. In the history of human cargo ships, only the "slave ships" and the "coffin ships" had worse conditions than army troop ships. The slave ships traveled the Atlantic Ocean in the 1800s and they carried hundreds of men, women, and children all huddled together in the crowded airless holds, teeming with disease, without light and virtually no food. The survivors of these ships were headed for a life of slavery in Europe or the United States. The "coffin ships" crossed the Atlantic from 1845 to 1850 and they carried up to a million Irish people during that time. The Irish were escaping the poverty and death resulting from the "Potato Famine" in Ireland, and they were heading for the United States and Canada in filthy, disease laden cargo vessels, that became know as "coffin ships." The death rates on the slave ships and coffin ships were very high.

In contrast to the troop ship conditions for enlisted men down in the holds, the officers, up to the grade of colonel and the higher ranking enlisted men of staff sergeant and above, were living in relative comfort in their staterooms above decks. These men even complained because they had to endure the indignity of sharing their stateroom with another officer. They ate in well appointed dining rooms and were served by enlisted men who waited on their every request. High level officers, full colonel and above, lived and dined as if they were on a first class luxury liner, and were waited on by enlisted men who served their every desire. "Yes, sir. Will there be anything else, sir?" "Steak not done to your liking, sir? Sorry about that, sir!" "We'll take care of that, sir." Of course, all the while these GI servants were muttering under their breath, "Go fuck yourself, sir." While the enlisted men below decks were eating greasy, dehydrated scrambled eggs, uncooked bacon, and shit on a shingle (SOS), that's dried out chipped beef swimming in greasy, creamed gravy—these high level officers were served steaks served to their preference, mashed potatoes or French fries, and then crème brulee for dessert. Troop ships that were used to transport enlisted men during World War II and the Korean War were excellent examples of the "caste system" that the army is famous for. These ships were nothing more than pathetic, overcrowded dungeons, and it was complete chaos down in the holds; men jammed in like sardines; nowhere to go except on deck where there was also no room to stand and nothing to do.

After all the troops were on board, the first thing that the officers ordered—was what is called in the army—a "short arm" inspection, in other words, a "pecker check" to see if any of the men had picked up a case of VD before getting on board. These men had been on leave before shipping out, and they wanted to get laid before heading to a war zone, so the army wanted to make sure that anyone with venereal disease was discovered and treated right away. All the men were ordered to their holds, told to strip and stand in line for this "pecker check." The medic sat in a chair with a flashlight while the soldiers passed before him one at a time. "Slide it back, and milk it down," was the order the medic gave to everyone in front of him, as he shined his flashlight on what was shown to him, looking for any discharge. Any soldier who didn't pass the "short arm" inspection was pulled out and sent to the infirmary. So there everyone was, standing around bare-ass in an overcrowded, unventilated hold, being very careful not to get too close to the guy next to you. Unless you have been there and experienced it, a pathetic situation like a "short arm" inspection in an overcrowded hold on a Victory ship can't be explained. And there is nothing to do on these troop ships except stand around in chow lines all day long, for meals that aren't worth eating. When the men weren't standing in a chow line, they were on kitchen police (KP) in the mess hall, or standing guard duty. There were also poker games going 24 hours a day and considerable money was changing hands.

The trip from California to Yokahama, Japan took 30 days, and no one was disappointed to get off those ships, even though they knew it was one step closer to the front line in Korea. The troop ship carrying Parker, Hansen and Foley arrived in Yokahama on September 25, 1950. They were then loaded onto army semis and transported to Camp Drake, a U.S. Army base outside Yokahama where they were processed and assigned to units in Korea.

Camp Drake may have been located in Japan but it was no different than army bases anywhere in the United States. The military police guarding the base; the army style barracks; the PX; the service clubs; the NCO clubs; the three point two beer; and the mess halls. One difference was the high fence that surrounded Camp Drake, making it more difficult for the enclosed GIs to go AWOL; but the high fence didn't stop these men when they knew that on the other side of the fence, every evening and lasting until daybreak, there were the ever present prostitutes. It didn't matter what country you were in, if you were an enlisted man on an army base, you had working girls outside the gate looking for company. An example in the United States was Camp Polk, Louisiana. The town outside Camp Polk was Leesville, but the GI name for Leesville, was Diseaseville.

Camp Drake was set up as a processing center and replacement depot for troops arriving from the United States. The length of stay at Camp Drake was anywhere from one week to ten days, long enough to check everyone's service record, give another "short arm" inspection to all the troops, and then send everyone off to Korea via Sasebo, Japan, a port city to the south that faced Pusan, Korea across the Korea Strait. In Sasebo the men were loaded onto army landing craft and carried across the straits to Pusan. Camp Drake was also the last chance that these GIs had to get out of the Korean pipeline. There were always rumors in the barracks about the severe battle conditions in Korea; about the hot and humid summers; about the drenching rainy season; about the mountainous and treacherous terrain; and about the deep snow and freezing temperatures in the winter. These rumors always presented conditions in the worst possible light, and although most of them would end up being true, the talk spread rapidly among the troops and only added to their anxiety. There were also rumors about military jobs that were available in Japan for those lucky enough to get them. All of these men were headed for combat with 8th Army infantry regiments, but that didn't stop them from hoping to be called out for a job as chaplain's assistant, or a general's driver, or a company clerk, or a supply clerk. None of these men would get jobs like these, but that didn't stop the rumors from spreading.

David Hansen and James Foley were processed through Camp Drake and assigned to infantry regiments in Korea. Michael Parker won a temporary reprieve from Korea by being selected for a slot in radio school. The 8th Army was in bad need of radio operators to improve communication on the battlefield. This radio school was a three month course and included extensive Morse code instruction and a complete orientation in radio procedure. The school was located on the island of Eta Jima, in southern Japan, not far from Hiroshima. Eta Jima was the former home of the Japanese Naval Academy, taken over by the U.S. Army after World War II, and converted into a large school in advanced communication. Michael Parker could not believe it when his name was called and he was told to report to the Eta Jima School Command. His commanding officer told him that he had done exceptionally well on the communication/Morse code part of the army I.Q. examination, and he had therefore been selected as a student in the next class of radio operators.

The army always maintained order by scheduling formations, assigning the troops to KP or guard duty, and they also conducted indoctrination classes regarding the enemy and Communism. These classes were designed to instill fear and hatred in the minds of the soldiers, and the classes included skits put on by NCOs and officers showing the suffering that the people who lived under Communism had to endure. The actors in these skits showed what the military wanted you to believe would happen to those living under Communist domination; families separated and sent to labor camps for no reason; citizens executed for crimes against the State; drastic living conditions; high unemployment; lack of food supplies; inadequate and inferior health care. These indoctrination classes were scheduled whenever the men had any free time, and they were presented frequently.

On October 15, David Hansen and James Foley arrived in Pusan, Korea. Pusan is the port city that every G.I. saw as he entered Korea. They had all heard rumors about the country, and about the mountains and bad weather. One of the rumors the GIs heard was that you could smell Korea 20 miles from its border. They heard and believed that human excrement was used as fertilizer because South Korea had no fertilizer source. At that time in Korean history, North Korea had all the power plants to make fertilizer and other products, whereas South Korea was the agrarian part of the country, the land for crops.

As Hansen and Foley disembarked from their LST, they were met by the army band that played military marching songs as the men were herded into a large amphitheater where they listened to a fighting pep talk by a high ranking officer. It was a speech that was supposed to instill the fighting spirit into the soldiers, and the officer ended his talk by shouting out, "You men have been called back to active duty to serve your country, and to defend our freedom. You have been sent to Korea to become killers, killers, killers!!!" These men, most of whom had served in combat in World War II, and whose morale at that point could not have been lower, responded by shouting a chorus of boos as the officer left the stage. "Your mother wears combat boots," someone shouted. "Why don't you court martial us, you asshole," another GI yelled, as the officer headed for the refuge of his company headquarters. After this session in the amphitheater, Hansen and Foley boarded buses that took them to a replacement depot outside Pusan. The buses wound through the broken streets of Pusan, streets with starving children milling around and chasing after the buses. These narrow streets were also crowded with refugees, sick and half clothed civilians, beggars, and the mutilated survivors of the war.

Hansen and Foley, and the other GIs on the bus looked out at the countryside, as their bus passed truck convoys heading toward the front lines, or the port of Pusan. There seemed to be smoke and dust everywhere, and the whole area seemed to be in a state of chaos.

After arriving at the replacement camp, the men got their gear and then were sent to a staging area and ordered to set up their pup tents. That night the rain was pouring down, heavy mud was everywhere—so after pitching the pup tent the soldiers had to dig a two foot trench around their tents to keep everything from being swept away in the flooding storm water. The next morning, while it was still dark, the men were called out in formation and told to respond to their name when their shipping orders were called off. When they heard their name called they were ordered to sound off with their last name and their serial number. If your name and shipping orders weren't called off during that formation, then you got to "sack out" on the cold, wet ground inside your pup tent until about 5 a.m. the next morning. Unless you've experienced the chaos and hopelessness in a wartime replacement depot, it can't be properly described.

The next morning Hansen and Foley got their unit assignment, and then were herded into a mess hall for breakfast. For breakfast you got GI coffee, grounds and all; dehydrated, greasy scrambled eggs; the old army standby "Shit on a Shingle," or SOS. After breakfast they were again called out in formation and boarded onto trucks for a ride to the train station; a train where these enlisted men were again jammed into boxcars like sardines, with their duffle bags and weapons, and told to maintain order for their train ride north past the 38th parallel to their unit assignment on the front line in North Korea. The trip to the train station went right through the city of Pusan, and there were large signs all along the streets advertising Korean women for sale. The signs stated, "Whorehouse—First Class," or "No. I Intercourse." In areas where the Military Police had tried to stop these activities, the signs read, "Laundry—24 Hour Service—formerly home of No. I Intercourse." There was always a Korean standing in front of the "Laundry" who was advertising the women inside.

Looking out of the truck, Hansen said, "Well, it looks like we won't be getting our laundry done on this trip."

"Well, maybe we can get it taken care of on the way back," Foley replied, taking in the same view from the truck of the "No. I Intercourse" building.

They looked at each other, and Hansen said, "Yeah, I hope we get the chance."

Once through the city and boarded onto the train, Foley and Hansen and the rest of the GIs, had to settle in for the 300 to 400 mile ride into North Korea. All along the way, the train served as an obvious target for North Korean snipers, as the train was shot at all along the way north toward the front lines. Finally, the troop train arrived at another replacement depot behind the front lines, where the men were assigned to their respective units.

# THE INCHON LANDING

In late July, as the last troops of General Walker's 8th Army were retreating south, they set up defensive positions after they crossed the Naktong River. General Walker told his troops at that time, "There will be no more retreating or withdrawal. These will be the lines beyond which we will not retreat. This is not going to be another Dunkirk or Bataan. A retreat to Pusan would be one of the greatest military disasters in history. We must fight to the end." It was during that time, when all the news from the front line was bad, that General Douglas MacArthur began planning for the Inchon landing behind enemy lines. However, while this planning was going on in Tokyo, the battle for the Pusan Perimeter under General Walker, was turning out to be the bloodiest battle of the Korean War, or any other war fought by the Americans. Military historians would rank the fighting around Pusan right up there with the worst of the Civil War battles, and with the bloody Pacific Island campaigns of World War II. As the pressure for victory mounted on both the Americans and the North Koreans—the Americans were rushing more and more troops to the battlefield. The American replacement troops, however, were not battle tested and were not eager for combat; they were actually sent as "cannon fodder" to stop the North Korean onslaught. Regardless, the tide of battle started to turn in the American's favor in late August 1950, although with huge casualties on both sides. The North Korean battle slogans at that time were, " Finish the battle before August" and "August must be the month of victory." These slogans reflected the growing fear among the North Korean leadership that the war now might turn into stalemate or defeat.

## THE KOREAN PIPELINE

The idea to land American troops at Inchon was actually first offered by General MacArthur on June 29, 1950, just four days after the war started. MacArthur predicted that the North Korean army would push the South Korean forces deep into South Korea, and he felt that an amphibious attack behind enemy lines at Inchon, at that time, would allow the Americans and Republic of Korea forces to cut off the North Korean Peoples Army and destroy them as a fighting force, thereby winning the war just weeks after the initial invasion.

However, this first Inchon landing strategy met with strong objections from other generals and the Joint Chiefs of Staff, mainly because of Inchon's natural defenses; namely, the restricted approaches to Inchon, the extensive mining of Inchon harbor, and the quick and changing currents in the channels. For these reasons, plus the formidable size and strength of the advancing North Korean army, General MacArthur and his advisors were forced to abandon his first Inchon landing operation. However, when the North Korean invasion pushed the Republic of Korea forces deep into South Korea and to the Pusan Perimeter, General MacArthur issued a revised plan of assault on Inchon, code-named Operation Chromite. The reason for the landing at Inchon included the fact that a successful amphibious attack and subsequent capture of Seoul would cut off the enemy supply lines and effectively encircle the enemy as they retreated from the Pusan Perimeter.

During this time, as the planning for the Inchon landing continued, MacArthur all but promised Washington, that a victory at Inchon would insure that the Americans would re-capture Seoul, the capital of Korea, just 90 days after it had been taken by North Korea. MacArthur stated, " The enemy has now concentrated more than 90 percent of his armed forces around the Pusan Perimeter and along the Naktong River; they are trying to drive General Walker and the 8th Army into the Korea Strait and the Sea of Japan." The Inchon beachhead, MacArthur stated, would demoralize and confuse the North Koreans, and allow General Walker to re-group and counter attack from the south, driving the North Koreans back past the 38th parallel.

There was extensive preparation and reconnaissance for the Inchon landing. Aerial photographs of Wolmi Island in Inchon harbor were taken which showed several batteries of North Korean gun emplacements. These were to be neutralized by naval gunfire and aerial bombing as the assault developed. A main concern about the landing at Inchon had to do with the timing of the tides in the harbor. An invasion at the wrong time could lead to grounded landing craft in the harbor and open the American amphibious force to the enemy artillery and ground attack. It was determined that the only day that the landing could be mounted was on the 15th of September. The United States forces started preliminary bombardment of Inchon harbor several days before September 15, and then on the day of the assault the bombardment resumed in full force. Then the 1st Marine Division swept over Wolmi Island and the troops went ashore and fought their way into Inchon. The preliminary bombardment of Wolmi Island and Inchon harbor had demoralized the North Korean defenses, and the Marines got ashore with relatively few casualties.

The battle of Inchon began on September 15 and ended on September 28. Before the invasion, American warplanes flew over the harbor islands, dropping a large number of napalm canisters in an effort to burn out the avenues of entrance into Inchon in an attempt to clear the way for American forces.

The American air bombardment was followed by an assault on Inchon harbor under the name of Task Force Seven. This Task Force included 320 warships and four aircraft carriers carrying 70,000 enlisted men into Inchon harbor. The attack plan included landing at three locations in the harbor, and they were designated as Green Beach, Red Beach and Blue Beach. In the early morning of September 15, the lead elements of X Corps hit Green Beach on the northern side of Wolmi-Do Island. The landing force consisted of the 3rd Battalion 5th Marines and nine M-26 Pershing tanks equipped with flame throwers and bulldozer blades. The entire island was taken by noon with light casualties on the American side. The North Korean casualties included more than 200 killed in action and 150 captured.

# THE KOREAN PIPELINE

In the afternoon of the 15th, after the tides had returned, the rest of the 5th Marines assaulted Red Beach, located northeast of Wolmi-Do Island, and they were able to open the Wolmi-Do causeway, and thereby allow tanks to enter the battle. Red Beach was taken by the 1st Marine regiment, under the command of Colonel Lewis "Chesty" Puller, and they were the last assault group to reach shore. By that time the North Korean resistance had been defeated due to the destroyer firepower and bombing runs conducted by the Americans. After reaching shore, the Marines strengthened their beachhead and prepared for the inland invasion and capture of Inchon.

Immediately after the North Korean defeat at Inchon, the Americans began the supply and troop reinforcement process. By September 19, the United States Corps of Engineers had repaired the local railroad up to ten miles toward Seoul, captured Kimpo airstrip near Inchon, and then transport planes began flying in ordnance and gasoline for aircraft stationed at the airstrip. By September 22, the United States Army had unloaded more than 6,000 vehicles, 54,000 troops, and over 25,000 tons of supplies to aid the American advance on the South Korean capital of Seoul.

# *BATTLE FOR SEOUL*

The battle to recapture Seoul, in contrast to the quick victory at Inchon, was slow and bloody. The U.S. Marines entered Seoul on September 22 and found it so heavily fortified that the advance on the capital city turned out to be slow, house-to-house, hand-to-hand combat. The North Koreans launched a T-34 tank attack and staged a YAK bombing run in an attempt to stall the United Nations advance on Seoul to allow time for their forces to withdraw from the Pusan Perimeter, and to defend the capital city. All of these actions resulted in fierce fighting around Seoul from September 19 through September 25. The X Corps commander, General Edward Almond, was in charge of the assault on Seoul, and he was anxious to announce the conquest of that city. Therefore, on September 25, despite the fact that the Marines were still engaged in house-to-house combat, General Almond declared the city liberated. It took several more days of intense fighting, however, before the city of Seoul was actually taken over by the Americans.

The amphibious landing at Inchon is considered to be one of the most decisive military operations in modern warfare. However, Russel Stolfi, in his writing in the Journal of Military History, "A Critique of Pure Success: Inchon Revisited, Revised, and Contrasted" in 2004, stated that although the landing at Inchon was strategically successful, it was followed by an advance on Seoul and a ground battle that was so slow and cautious that it constituted "an operational disaster," that largely negated the success at Inchon harbor. Regardless, most military historians report that the landing at Inchon was quick and successful, and although the advance on Seoul which followed was slow and tentative, and resulted in heavy casualties, the American forces prevailed, and by

# THE KOREAN PIPELINE

September 28, 1950 the South Korean capital city was liberated. This recapture of Seoul severed the North Korean Peoples Army supply lines and thereby placed the enemy forces remaining in South Korea in a dangerously indefensible position. The landing at Inchon, then, resulted in a decisive victory, a much needed victory, that set the stage for a strategic reversal in the course of the Korean War in favor of the United Nations. This reversal in fortune was slated for a very short duration.

General MacArthur, at night following the success at Inchon, on-board his headquarters ship Mount McKinley, dined with his senior staff commanders. They were in an arrogant, festive, and jingoistic mood. MacArthur now felt, after this campaign success, that Washington and President Truman, would find it impossible to challenge his authority. Although the Inchon landing was successful and allowed General Walker to hold the Pusan Perimeter and then head north, the events and battles that followed, along with General MacArthur's fateful decisions, would lead to unforeseen and tragic consequences.

## *RUSH TO THE YALU RIVER*

After the success at Inchon, the 8th Army broke out from the Pusan Perimeter and headed north. Although the North Korean Peoples Army fought isolated rear guard action to delay the advancing Americans, it became clear to them that they had sustained a major setback at Inchon, and needed to withdraw deep into North Korea. Back in Washington, the question of whether to cross the 38th parallel, and head north toward the Yalu River, became paramount. Many politicians, mainly those of the infamous China Lobby, demanded that the United States offensive continue into enemy territory. Senator William Knowland of California, one of the China Lobby's most ardent spokesmen, was already accusing those who called for stopping at the 38th parallel as appeasers, if not traitors. Many of these hardliners complained that since the Communists had started the war; and since so many Americans had already died in Korea; and since MacArthur, the commander in the field (although he had never spent one night in Korea), wanted to go north to the Yalu and perhaps beyond to Manchuria; that therefore, the decision to cross the 38th parallel and head north was preordained.

The political forces that were advocating that the 8th Army should cross the 38th parallel were simply too strong to be denied. Those that considered this policy to be extremely dangerous were led by George Kennan, a well known expert on Russian and Chinese affairs. However, Kennan's influence in the Truman administration had been systematically eroded by Dean Rusk, then Deputy Secretary of State, and who would eventually become a notorious hardliner on Asian Communism. At that time, most of the Congress and a majority of the

American public (64 percent according to a Gallup poll taken in October 1950), wanted to pursue the North Koreans beyond the 38th parallel. Also, by the time that the Truman administration faced this decision, George Kennan and his supporters, were no longer major players in the administration. They had told Truman that crossing the parallel and trying to unite Korea would make the United States the aggressor, and would present a great risk that the Chinese and possibly the Russians would enter the war. Kennan was sure that the United States was headed for a major military crisis, and that allowing MacArthur free rein in Korea would lead to disaster. He felt that the United States was over-reaching militarily for a geopolitical gain that was not important to our safety as a nation. Although George Kennan was not able to influence the Truman administration, his predictions turned out to be all too correct. In the few months that followed the United States crossing of the 38th parallel, thousands more American, South Korean, North Korean and Chinese men would be slaughtered in the frigid, barren mountains of North Korea.

The successful defense of the Pusan Perimeter followed by the American amphibious assault at Inchon brought the United Nations forces back from near defeat to the brink of victory. If General MacArthur had stopped there, after that battlefield success, he would still be regarded as that "mythical genius," that hero of the Pacific Campaign in World War II who was now declaring the Korean War over in less than three months. In the weeks that followed the Inchon landing, however, the battle decisions made by General MacArthur, and left unchallenged by the Truman administration, would lead to a prolonged war with no victory in sight, and would place in stark doubt his competency in making these decisions.

While the North Korean Peoples Army was fighting in Pusan, their overextended supply lines were attacked daily by American airpower. After Inchon, these vulnerable supply lines forced the enemy to withdraw back north in full retreat. It was at this time that the United States 8th Army had the opportunity to exploit the success at Inchon by cutting off the enemy retreat and destroying the remaining North Korean forces. Instead of following this battle plan, MacArthur began preparing the 8th Army and the X Corps for another amphibious landing at Wonsan, a port city on the east coast of Korea. This MacArthur decision wasted valuable time as he repositioned his forces and planned a second amphibious attack. The resulting failure of General MacArthur to join the forces of the 8th Army and X Corps, and thereby cut off the retreating North Koreans, allowed an estimated 30,000 to 40,000 enemy infantrymen to escape back to North Korea.

Military historians have harshly criticized General MacArthur's decisions after the Inchon landing, but they have not laid the blame entirely on the General. The Truman administration and the Joint Chiefs of Staff were so impressed by the success at Inchon, that they hesitated to question his later decisions and battle plans. In General Ridgeway's book "The Korean War" he wrote:

"A more subtle result of the Inchon triumph was the development of an almost superstitious regard for General MacArthur's infallibility. Even his supervisors, it seemed, began to doubt if they should question any of MacArthur's decisions, and as a result, he was deprived of the advantage of forthright and informal criticism—"

This statement by General Ridgway in his book about the Korean War confirmed what many military historians have written about General MacArthur; that the success at Inchon only increased his jingoistic aggressiveness, as well as his disregard and lack of respect for the enemy. He became supremely confident and saw himself as that great American General who was destined to defeat global Communism. After Inchon, General MacArthur renewed his battlefield plans to include the unification of Korea, and to head into Manchuria and defeat the Chinese, should they enter the war. In the months to come, however, General MacArthur and the American 8th Army would be overwhelmed by hundreds of thousands of Chinese soldiers, and United Nations forces would be forced to withdraw back to a position below the 38th parallel.

*THE KOREAN PIPELINE*

MAC ARTHUR SAYS YOU'VE GOT TO ATTACK
BUT YOU FOLLOW MAC AND YOU'LL NEVER COME BACK
WE'RE MOVING ON, WE'RE MOVING ON
YOU FOLLOW MAC AND YOU'LL NEVER COME BACK
WE'RE MOVING ON.

President Truman, certainly influenced by his renewed confidence in General MacArthur, ordered that United States forces should cross the 38th parallel and defeat what was remaining of the North Korean Peoples Army. This was a new cause of action for the United States, and was not authorized by the initial United Nations resolution that sent in United Nations forces. The United Nations resolution that supported intervention in Korea stated that the objectives were to force the North Korean Peoples Army out of South Korea, and to restore the original border between the two Koreas. The new decision by the Truman administration was aimed at completely destroying the North Korean Peoples Army, and then unifying Korea under one government.

While General Walker and his 8th Army advanced north from the Pusan Perimeter after Inchon, the Republic of Korea Army (South Korea) was also heading north along the east coast. The unification of Korea was also on the mind of Syngman Rhee, the President of South Korea, when he stated on September 19, 1950, at a meeting in Pusan, that he did not expect the United Nations forces to stop at the 38th parallel. He ordered his Republic of Korea Army to "advance all the way to the Manchurian border in order to rid the country of enemy soldiers." Syngman Rhee was never shy about expressing his desire to unify Korea under his presidency. By October 13, all ROK divisions and part of the 8th Army were across the 38th parallel and had advanced on the Iron Triangle in the Central Corridor of Korea, and had also secured the eastern port city of Wonsan.

Some military historians note that General MacArthur did not take advantage of the favorable positions occupied by his forces in October 1950. United Nations forces, at that time, had the opportunity to control a defensive line across the narrowest portion of the Korean peninsula.

From that position General Walker's 8th Army could have cut off the retreating NKPA forces and destroyed a major part of their army. This plan might also have prevented the entry of Chinese forces into the Korean War. If General MacArthur had limited his advance to a latitude between Wonsan and Pyongyang, then the Chinese would not have been able to claim that United States forces were threatening its borders, and, therefore, would not have entered the war.

What actually happened, however, was that General MacArthur, overstepping the authorization he received from the Joint Chiefs of Staff, not only crossed the 38th parallel but he ordered his troops to continue north to a position only 30 to 40 miles south of the Yalu River and the Manchurian border. This was contrary to what was authorized by the Joint Chiefs of Staff, but General MacArthur justified his position by claiming it was a military necessity. While MacArthur was ordering his troops to advance into the northern part of Korea close to the Manchurian border, the Chinese government was protesting at the United Nations that American forces were threatening their borders. The Chinese government made explicit warnings at the United Nations that military advances on their territory would result in retaliatory action.

General MacArthur ignored these verbal warnings at the United Nations, and stated that he did not believe these "threats" would be carried out by the Chinese government. The Chinese also faced down American forces at Unsan in late October 1950, in a battle that was called "The Warning at Unsan" by David Halberstam in his novel "The Coldest Winter." This was a devastating defeat for the American forces, but did nothing to stop General MacArthur, as he ignored the Chinese warning at Unsan, and pressed his troops north to the Yalu River. As it turned out, the Chinese army formally entered the war in late November 1950, causing heavy casualties to American forces and forcing them to withdraw south of the Chongchon River, and eventually back to the 38th parallel.

The decision to cross the 38th parallel into North Korea was made in late September 1950 and as the North Korean People's Army retreated there were intelligence reports that the Chinese were massing along the Manchurian border, getting closer to intervention. Then on September

30, just two weeks after Inchon, the South Korean 2nd Infantry Division crossed into North Korea; then, a week later on October 7, troops from the American 1st Cavalry Division crossed the 38th parallel also. They went on to capture Pyongyang, the capitol of North Korea, and headed for the Yalu River and the Manchurian border, as the weather turned bitterly cold and the snow began to fall. Right after that in early November, the 1st Cavalry had their first battle with the formidable Chinese army at Unsan. Unfortunately, it would not be their last encounter with the Chinese Communists.

THE SNOW'S COMING DOWN, IT'S FREEZING TOO
AND NOW WE'RE OFF TO THE BIG YALU
WE'RE MOVING ON, WE'RE MOVING ON
IT'S STARTING TO SNOW, WE'VE GOT TO GO
WE'RE MOVING ON

## THE BATTLE AT UNSAN

Corporal David Hansen boarded a troop train in Pusan for the journey north past the 38$^{th}$ parallel. The trip from Pusan to their destination in North Korea lasted two days. It should have been a shorter trip but the train moved slowly and made many stops along the way. They were also subjected to sniper fire from North Korean troops that had been by-passed by the Americans as they headed north. These enemy troops bivouacked in the hills and mountains as the Americans went by; then they would stage rear guard attacks on American forces, but they were soon routed out and did not stop the American advance. Although the train made many stops as it headed north, the troops on board did not choose to leave the train when it stopped, as they had on their train trip across the United States. They knew that leaving the train in Korea would leave them with no good options.

David Hansen arrived at the headquarters of the U.S. 1$^{st}$ Cavalry Division in early October 1950, and was assigned to an infantry company. Before reporting for duty Hansen completed three days of combat training back at Danger Rear, where the training consisted mainly of firing weapons and bayonet warfare. They were instructed during their training that while they were on guard duty or on patrol, that often many Koreans (always referred to as Gooks) would approach the Americans dressed in long white civilian garments. The men were told that if they attempted to take these "civilians" as prisoners of war, that as soon as the Koreans got close enough to the Americans they would open their white civilian garments and open fire on them with their Chinese burp guns. Although it was never stated that you should shoot these Koreans, it was made clear that if you attempted to take any prisoners you were taking your life in you own hands. After completing this course in front line combat, no one planned to take any prisoners of war.

On October 20, the 1st Cav moved into and captured Pyongyong, the North Korean capital. To the men of the 1st Cavalry the capture of the North Korean capital meant that the war was almost over. The troops were ecstatic and everyone was talking about getting out of Korea, going back to Japan and then on to the United States. Some members of the 1st Cav were roaming through the capital city, painting the 1st Cav logo on buildings all over town. They wanted everyone that followed them into Pyongyang, to know that the 1st Cavalry Division was the first to enter and liberate Pyongyang. The rumors that the war was almost over kept spreading, and then a request came from company headquarters asking all men with ship loading experience to notify their superiors, a sure sign to the men that they would soon begin to withdraw and prepare to ship out. They had also been told to turn in most of their ammunition. Soon rumors began circulating among the men about a victory parade being planned that was to take place in Tokyo. The 1st Cavalry was reported to be General MacArthur's favorite unit and they would be selected to lead the parade.

On top of all this optimism, it turned out that Bob Hope, the famous comedian well known for entertaining the troops, was going to put on a show in the North Korean capital. That night the men of the 1st Cav gathered on the side of a Korean hill, sitting on their helmets, drinking their beer ration and whatever whiskey they had hidden, and watched the Bob Hope show. The next morning, many of the men still hung over from drinking while watching the entertainment, the company was mobilized for what they were told would be their last patrol in Korea. They were ordered to a village just north of Pyongyang, a place called Unsan. Although Unsan was located on the Yalu River dangerously close to the Manchurian border, these troops never felt as if they were in harm's way as they headed north. They were in a good mood, Bob Hope and the bevy of beautiful girls in his show were still on their minds, and as they moved from Pyongyang to Unsan they felt that they were wiping out the last remnants of a defeated North Korean army. The troops were very confident, and a certain euphoria was spreading among the ranks. The men were even joking about reaching the Yalu, and taking a leak in the river as a personal sign of triumph. When the 1st Cavalry reached Unsan the commander sent out a patrol to a position about five miles north of their CP. The patrol came upon a Korean farmer who told them that there were thousands of heavily armed Chinese infantrymen in the area, many of whom had arrived on horseback. The mood among the troops changed immediately from euphoria to tension, and fear of what might lie ahead. They had no way of knowing that by November 1, 1950, the 1st Cavalry would be completely encircled by Chinese forces, and that when the ensuing battle was over, the troops of the 1st Cav would not be taking a leak in the Yalu River as a personal sign of triumph—but they would have suffered the worst defeat of the Korean War up to that time.

The Chinese, who had been massing along the Manchurian border, attacked in early November and completely surrounded the American forces. When it was all over, there were more than 1000 American casualties among the estimated 2200 men in the regiment. This encounter with the Chinese Communists was disastrous for American morale. Just when they thought that the war was ending, and that the 1st Cavalry would be leading a victory parade in Tokyo, the Chinese Communists showed up in force and handed an elite American regiment a demoralizing defeat. The 1st Cavalry lost half their strength at Unsan, including most of its equipment, artillery, tanks, trucks, and weapons. According to one battlefield reporter, " The Chinese attack at Unsan was an Indian style attack, like the one that defeated General Custer at Little Big Horn."

When David Hansen arrived for duty with the 1st Cavalry, the mood among the troops was one of exhaustion, yet they were optimistic. Hansen had already heard the worst about the battles at the Pusan Perimeter, but when he listened to the rumors about Thanksgiving and Christmas in the States, he began to feel that the worst was behind them. However, he also noticed that in the evening the enemy fire and mortars were increasing in intensity. They also began to hear for the first time what to them sounded like bagpipes. They actually began to think that British reinforcements had arrived to help secure victory against the enemy. However, it was not bagpipes they heard, and it was not British reinforcements; instead it was the strange, eerie, foreign sound of bugles and flutes; a sound they would remember for the rest of their lives. These musical sounds were used by the Chinese for many reasons. The sound of the bugles and trumpets were a call to action for the Chinese infantry, signifying a time to enter battle. These sounds were also meant to strike fear into the hearts of the Americans. Later in the war, after the Chinese had officially entered the conflict, these bugles would sound at night, always before a Chinese attack. The Chinese also used loudspeakers before an attack; loudspeakers that would blare out to the American troops slogans such as, "Tonight, Americans you die," that sounded like "Tonigh, Amellican, you die!" and "You should be home GI, not here," and "Tonight GI, you die, so far from home." Then the bugles would blow; followed by a massive Chinese attack.

Corporal Hansen was assigned to Headquarters Company as a runner and communications contact man. His job was to deliver messages, oral and written, from Battalion Headquarters to the line companies. It was very dangerous duty, and Hansen knew that the enemy always targeted radiomen and communication runners. His assignment caused him to spend a lot of time around Headquarters Company, so he heard a lot of what the high levels officers were saying. Major General Hap Gay, the 1st Cavalry commanding officer at that time, took the intelligence reports of Chinese infantry in the area, very seriously, and on November 1 his command post was set up just south of Unsan. General Gay felt as though his unit was open to enemy attack from all sides. It is reported that General Gay was furious at the way the 8th Army had been fighting the Korean War. He felt that everything had been done wrong, right from the start. He also felt that his superiors in Tokyo had little knowledge or respect for the enemy, or for the Korean terrain. After General Gay had received a briefing at MacArthur's Headquarters in Tokyo, he is reported to have told his administrative officer, "Those goddamn people in Tokyo don't have their feet on the ground, they're living in a goddamn dream world." As Corporal Hansen listened to the officers at the CP, he realized that his regiment jutted out on point and was very vulnerable from all sides should there be an enemy attack.

Another problem that the United States army faced was the large number of poorly trained South Korean soldiers that were attached to American units. Most American officers felt they could not rely on these soldiers; they also felt that these South Koreans were attached to their units only to make the United Nations forces look stronger on paper than they actually were. This battlefield experiment only made matters worse since the American soldiers who fought along side the Koreans could not communicate with them, and many times, because of battlefield paranoia, were not sure if these men were South Korean or North Korean.

Late in the evening of November 1, the Chinese bugles and trumpets began to sound off, and then the Chinese attacked, sending wave after wave of infantrymen through the American defensive perimeter. The American units were so thinly spread out that the Chinese met very little resistance as they spearheaded across the fragile American defenses. The Americans were shell shocked in more ways than one. They had actually believed the rumors of their returning to the United States as a victorious army—and now they seemed to be facing an overwhelming defeat. Corporal Hansen was not prepared for this type of warfare; virtually face to face with the enemy in hand-to-hand combat. It seemed to Hansen as if the Chinese were racing through their perimeter defenses as if they were at a track meet; breaking through their lines and then spreading out among the Americans firing their weapons at random. Some of the survivors of the initial attack tried to form a second perimeter, but they were quickly overrun. There were dead and wounded soldiers everywhere, and chaos was spreading among the American troops. The army trucks that were available began loading as many wounded as they could, preparing to head for the rear, but as the survivors headed south out of Unsan, they were in complete disarray, many without their weapons or grenades. Many front line units and artillery companies had stopped issuing hand grenades to the troops, except during a combat emergency. The problem they were attempting to avoid was that when combat pressure slackened, many soldiers discarded their hand grenades into unit trucks or jeeps. The subsequent movement of the vehicles would often shake the grenade pins loose, resulting in explosions that caused severe troop injuries and damage to equipment.

The Chinese had set up a formidable force on both sides of the Unsan road, waiting to ambush the Americans. As the retreating American army passed through the ambush area, the Chinese opened fire, and their firepower was devastating. The American convoy had to slow down and then come to a stop, and the American soldiers were forced to wait there, with no means of fighting back, as the Chinese infantry fired down on them from all sides.

Corporal Hansen was among the survivors at that point, lying among the dead and wounded on the battlefield, and he felt that the only chance he had was to play dead, as the Chinese walked over the dead and wounded, beating them with their rifle butts and bayoneting many of them. He waited there for hours, afraid to move, and then, slowly, he started to crawl away. Hansen was completely disoriented, weak from dehydration, suffering from his wounds and, in the darkness of night, he had no idea which way would lead him back to what was left of his company. Then he heard artillery fire in the distance, and saw the flashing lights from the howitzers, and he assumed they were Americans, so he headed that way.

What happened at Unsan, the Chinese warning of what was to come, turned out to be just the beginning. Even more disastrous battles were to follow three weeks later as the Americans followed General MacArthur's orders and moved closer to the Yalu River and the Manchurian border; battles that would pit the American and United Nations forces, who were completely unprepared for what was to come, against a formidable Chinese army, in freezing weather and under severe ground conditions that only favored the Chinese.

# THE TRUMAN ADMINISTRATION AND GENERAL MACARTHUR: NOVEMBER, DECEMBER 1950

Back in the United States, the American public did not hear about the battle at Unsan. The press was more concerned with MacArthur's optimistic statements regarding victory in Korea, parades in Japan, and the troops coming home for Thanksgiving and Christmas. President Truman and his advisors, however, knew all about the bad news coming out of Korea, and had been concerned for weeks about a possible Chinese intervention into the war. When they received the report about the American rout at Unsan at the hands of the Chinese, President Truman and his advisors seemed to be in a state of paralysis, not able to make a decision. The Joint Chiefs of Staff called MacArthur on November 3, 1950, and asked him for a response to what had happened at Unsan, an overt intervention by the Chinese Communists. The following few days demonstrated the difference in strategy between Washington (President Truman and the Joint Chiefs of Staff) and General MacArthur. MacArthur made it known that he wanted to forge ahead to the Yalu River, and even beyond into Manchuria if he deemed it necessary, to defeat the Chinese Communists. He wanted to defeat the North Koreans and the Chinese, and thereby unify Korea and defeat global Communism. He also left open the threat of using atomic weapons. On the other hand, President Truman and his advisors, wanted no part of a major war with China. They saw MacArthur's strategy as leading to disaster, opening the real possibility not only of a war with China and Russia, but also the potential start of World War III.

General MacArthur, it has been reported, also deliberately minimized or misinterpreted both the intentions and the size of the Chinese forces. By November 3, 1950, after the warning at Unsan, MacArthur placed the number of Chinese troops in Korea at about 20,000. In reality, and this according to intelligence available to MacArthur, there were more than 300,000 Chinese infantrymen, roughly 30 divisions, already in Korea. MacArthur may have been surprised and shaken by the assault at Unsan, but he brazenly downplayed its importance in his reporting to Washington. MacArthur also is reported to have said that he had "no respect for these Chinese laundrymen." And he had previously referred to Kim Il Sung, the North Korean Communist leader, as "Kim Buck Tooth," in a mocking, racist reference to the North Korean leader and his nation. Were these the statements of "The Great One," the mythical American general who had "saved" America from defeat in the Pacific at the hands of the Japanese in World War II, or was he in reality a right wing jingoistic ideologue, and a racist, even though he had lived in Japan for the previous five years.

Historians have come down on both sides of General MacArthur's legacy. On the one hand he was the brilliant leader willing to take chances that were often successful battle campaigns; on the other hand, he was the meglamaniac general, more concerned with his own resume and his charisma, someone willing to order bizarre campaign moves that often resulted in failure. In both the former and the latter cases, the enlisted men under General MacArthur, the men on the ground, were the ones who paid for MacArthur's blunders, as they were the ones who suffered and died. The soldiers who had to follow General MacArthur's orders had slogans about how they felt about him. "Follow Mac and you'll never come back," was one you heard over and over again. And there were variations on this slogan that added more basic and descriptive words about their feelings regarding MacArthur. As a matter of fact, the low esteem with which MacArthur was held by his troops, permeated throughout the ranks. The enlisted men not only hated most of their officers, they did not trust them. The enlisted men felt as if the officers spent all of their time back in Danger Rear, that safe haven behind the front lines, where the officers spent their time reading maps and checking coordinates, and devising maneuvers that were sure to result in more dead American soldiers. The enlisted men saw the officers as those sitting back at the Command Post adding battle stars to their resume, dividing up unearned medals (medals that should have been distributed among the enlisted men in their company), and seldom showing up on the front lines. When the officers did visit the front, they made sure it was in the morning, because they knew that the North Koreans and the Chinese only attacked at night.

If MacArthur had been somewhat taken aback by the Chinese attack at Unsan, he quickly rationalized away that defeat, and became even more confident once again. However, General Walton Walker, who commanded the United States 8th Army, whose troops had been run over at the Pusan Perimeter, and again at Unsan, sent a cable to General MacArthur's headquarters in Tokyo stating that they had sustained an ambush and surprise attack by fresh, well organized and well trained units, most of which were Communist Chinese forces.

This message of candor from General Walker did not please Douglas MacArthur, who wanted to minimize the Chinese threat. MacArthur wanted to continue to push northward, to conduct the campaign as if all were well. He threatened to relieve General Walker from command, and asked him why he had broken off contact with the enemy at Unsan. MacArthur asked General Walker why he had retreated to behind the Chongchon River; pushed back, as MacArthur put it, by a few Chinese volunteers. He told General Walker that he was failing as an Army commander.

On November 6, 1950, MacArthur, apparently confident of his assessment of the battlefield situation, sent a message to Washington stating that the Korean War was practically over and that a unified Korea was within reach. The Truman Administration, however, had a very different view. Truman and the Joint Chiefs of Staff, by now close to the end of their rope with MacArthur, saw the defeat at Unsan as a showing of China's war potential, and they wanted to avoid a confrontation with them on their border.

General MacArthur, in the meantime, continued to send optimistic reports back to Washington from his headquarters in Japan. His recommendation, as it always had been, was to continue the drive northward toward the Yalu River, with the goal of conquering all of Korea. The danger to his troops from this formidable new enemy was ignored by MacArthur, thereby putting his army and men at great risk.

Back in Washington, the Truman Administration and his advisors, including Secretary of State Dean Acheson, seemed unable to take action. It now seemed that the conduct of the Korean War was being controlled by MacArthur's decision to move the American Army northward regardless of risk, and without regard for what the Chinese reaction to MacArthur's strategy would be. Dean Acheson warned President Truman that the moment was critical. He pointed out that the enemy had shown up on the battlefield as if from nowhere, had fought bravely, and then seemed to have vanished from the face of the earth. Acheson recommended that the United States use extreme caution, for he felt that the Chinese forces would probably reappear again, as suddenly and as harmfully as they had before.

In a related battle on November 2-4, at Sudong, on the east coast of Korea, the Marines who were a part of the X Corps, had been hit very hard in a battle that was very similar to the one at Unsan. During the Sudong battle, the marines lost more than 50 men killed in action and almost 200 wounded. Their intelligence told them that the attack had been well planned, and that it seemed as if the Chinese military leaders were baiting the Americans into a trap, and that they anticipated that the Americans would move farther north into their ambush. These intelligence reports would prove to be true as future battles between Chinese and United States forces developed, and would not be to the advantage of the Americans.

The results of the battles at Unsan and Sudong proved to be the last chance for the American forces to break off the drive north, to move back and further assess the situation, and to avoid a larger and very costly war with the Chinese. Faced with these battlefield conditions, and an out of control General MacArthur in Tokyo running a huge gamble in Korea, Washington did nothing. As Dean Acheson noted in his memoir, "We sat around like paralyzed rabbits, while MacArthur carried out his nightmare."

PART IV
THE CHINESE STRIKE: NOVEMBER, DECEMBER, 1950
THE CHONGCHON RIVER AND THE BATTLE OF KUNURI
THE SHOOTOUT AT CHINAMEN'S HAT
CHOSIN RESERVOIR
GENERAL RIDGWAY REPLACES GENERAL WALKER
RIDGWAY'S BATTLES: CHIPYONGU, WONJU. DECEMBER 1950-MARCH 1951

# *THE CHONGCHON RIVER AND THE BATTLE AT KUNURI*

Sergeant James Foley reported for duty on November 15, 1950 to the 9th Infantry Regiment of the 8th Army. When he joined his unit, the 9th Infantry Regiment was deployed along the Chongchon River, a shallow, broad river which flows across the northwestern part of the Korean peninsula to the Yellow Sea. The Chinese Communist Army, in the meantime, was massing along the northern border of the Chongchon River. The Chinese Army moved at night, and seemed to stay under the radar of U.S. intelligence. It is reported that they moved as if they were a phantom army, casting only a shadow, and maintaining secrecy about its strength, position, and intention.

So it was into these ominous circumstances, two armies confronting each other along the Chongchon River in North Korea, that Sergeant Foley reported for duty. Of all the units of the 8th Army that engaged the Chinese in November and December of 1950, it was the 9th Infantry Regiment that was the first to fight and the last to yield ground that it had taken—and as a result the 9th took heavy casualties.

On the morning of November 25, Thanksgiving Day for the Americans, the 9th Infantry Regiment of which Sgt. Foley was a part, headed north toward the Yalu River. They were following the orders of General MacArthur, who on November 24, as he faced various news reporters back in Tokyo, made one of his many home-before-Christmas statements. "You can tell the troops that when they get to the Yalu, they can all come home. I want to make good on my statement that they will get Christmas dinner at home." These statements were made by MacArthur at a time when he was completely aware of the recent battles at Unsan and Sudong, that warned of massive Chinese intervention if the U.S. forces moved north toward the Manchurian border. Regardless of these intelligence reports, MacArthur ordered his troops northward.

General Walton Walker, who at this time was still in command of the 8th Army, thought MacArthur was making campaign advances that were unwarranted and dangerous, and would force the Chinese to take action. Walker never questioned MacArthur in his presence, however, and before the 8th Army headed north on November 25, Walker visited Division headquarters near the front and told the commander of the 9th Infantry Regiment, one of the lead units in the drive north, "The first time you smell Chinese chow—pull back immediately."

Sergeant James Foley was unaware of the perilous situation his regiment faced. As a matter of fact, none of the enlisted men had any idea where they were, except that they were north of the 38th parallel. The men in the regiment had heard only the rumors about being home for Christmas, or at least being in Japan for the holidays. During the days before November 25, resistance to the advancing 9th Regiment had been light, and then suddenly the number of engagements with the enemy began to increase. Therefore, as they moved northward the confidence that the troops had been feeling began to give way to constant tension. The men now knew that their unit was virtually "on point" for the entire 8th Army.

Sergeant Foley was in constant contact with the 9th Regiment commander, and they both felt that their forces were positioned reasonably well. They knew that their battalion was not too spread out and that they were on relatively high ground; they felt confident that under "normal" battle conditions they could support one another. But there was nothing normal about what happened on the night of November 25. After dark that night, with bugles and trumpets blaring and loudspeakers sounding off, the Chinese attacked at several locations along the shallow Chongchon River. The eastern flank of the 9th Regiment, composed of Republic of Korea forces, collapsed almost immediately, and United States units were hit on all sides by wave after wave of Chinese infantrymen swarming all over them. Then later, after midnight, the attack seemed to increase in intensity. Reports began coming in to U.S. command headquarters from field battalions, and all of these reports were strident, with shock evident in every word: "We're holding—but they're all over the place," "My God, they're everywhere!!" "Every time we stop them, there are more of them," and "This may be our last message." And the soldiers giving the messages kept changing, as the battalion radiomen were hit. There was no way that the 9th Regiment, isolated as it was and with virtually no communication, could evaluate what was happening; everyone was shocked and disoriented; and with no orders coming from command headquarters, it was every man for himself. The commander of the regiment along with Sergeant Foley, however, maintained their calm, and did their best to move what remained of their regiment back to Danger Rear, where they hoped that they could regroup and form a defensive perimeter.

The entry into the Korean War by the Chinese Communists on that night, at several locations along the Chongchon River in late November 1950, was a disaster for the Americans. According to the military, there are different levels of military disasters. These levels depend upon battlefield conditions, leadership, and of course, the enemy. Some military situations are bad, but at least they are temporary; other situations happen because the unit is poorly positioned and/or poorly led; other battlefield conditions can develop as the retreating army moves their men around to protect those under attack. However, this battle was an entirely different kind of attack and disaster, and it grew worse by the hour. During those early hours on November 25 and 26, several companies of 8th Army infantry regiments were virtually wiped out. When one company fell, the pressure on adjacent units became indefensible, and that company retreated as well. It was almost like falling dominoes.

After the first offensive by the enemy, the survivors of the 9th Regiment led by a 1st Lieutenant and by Sergeant Foley, began to regroup back at Danger Rear near the village of Kunuri. Kunuri was south of the Chongchon River and about 50 miles from Unsan, the site of the first warning battle with the Chinese. The next evening, November 26, the Chinese struck at midnight, shocking the Americans by blowing bugles and trumpets. Immediately after the bugles sounded, the Chinese again advanced in waves, and suddenly they were right in the midst of the Americans. Sergeant Foley tried to rally his men, and they managed to hold for a short time before retreating again. The conditions on the ground were terrible, it was freezing cold; everyone was disoriented; it was a soldier's nightmare. There were dead and wounded everywhere, and the Americans were trying to clear their comrades off the battlefield. The regiment managed to struggle back, and they began to regroup with their battalion. By now all the survivors were banding together, but no one seemed to be in charge, and scenes like this were taking place throughout the 8th Army that night all along the Chongchon River. In this chaotic battlefield situation, the men were stumbling toward the rear, disoriented in the darkness, yet still hoping to find refuge with other survivors.

**YOU HEAR THE RUMBLE OF RUNNING FEET**
**THE 24TH DIVISION IS IN FULL RETREAT**
**WE'RE MOVING ON, WE'RE MOVING ON**
**CHINESE BUGLES BLOW, WE'VE GOT TO GO**
**WE'RE MOVING ON**

Finally, the next morning, the Chinese relented and the men of the 9th Regiment reached the bank of a tributary of the Chongchon River where they regrouped and joined the survivors of the 38th Infantry Regiment. By then they had picked up two more tanks which seemed to offer them a feeling of safety and security; however, it would turn out to be a false security.

Back in Kunuri, it was as if no one was in charge. Everyone seemed to be lost, and dazed from battle fatigue, no one able to give a coherent command. Sergeant Foley now knew that the entire Division, not just the 9th Regiment, was in dire jeopardy. By November 29, every soldier in Kunuri knew that the Chinese Communists were advancing closer every hour, and that the situation for U.S. forces was going from bad to worse. At that time in the battle everything favored the Chinese. There were so many of them; their supply lines were short; they could continuously re-supply weapons and infantry; and they could block the avenues of retreat for U.S. forces.

Sergeant Foley, his company commander and survivors of the 9th Regiment, managed to reconnoiter at Kunuri. They knew that the Chinese were pressing in all around them, and they were in danger of losing not only their regiment, but the whole division. There were so many Chinese troops that they were able to block the avenues of Allied forces retreat, and then tighten the noose around them as they tried to withdraw. To add to the confusion, no one seemed to know where the Chinese were coming from, or how many of them there were. Also, no one had any idea of what their main or secondary route to the south should be. It was total bedlam; with no one in charge; no one knew north from south; and the American soldiers didn't know a South Korean from a North Korean. Again, through no fault of the American soldier on the ground, it was total chaos on the battlefield.

In the days following the retreat from Kunuri, Sergeant Foley knew that it was going to be bad. The Chinese were able to effectively move at night, slip around the American lines, and then isolate them from their support. The front line was still very far north; the roads were narrow and icy, making it extremely difficult, if not impossible, to supply their units; and there was virtually no communication among the front line units. Radiomen were often the first to be targeted by the Chinese, and the short supply of competent radiomen was always a problem. And after the success of the first Chinese offensive became apparent, the "myth of battle" suddenly favored the Chinese. There were such large numbers of them; they were fanatical and fearless (at least the American soldiers thought they were); and they fought brilliantly at night after having surrounded a United Nations position before a shot was fired. Initially, the fear factor of war had favored the Americans; the fear of a vastly superior American army and weaponry; not to mention their air superiority and the use of the dreaded napalm. However, now the voices of fear and panic swept over the men of the 8th Army. General MacArthur and his advisors in Tokyo had greatly under-estimated the military capabilities of the Chinese army, and these capabilities were now magnified, and terrorizing the American troops on the ground.

On the battlefield there may be nothing worse than the fear of the unknown, the loneliness that the front line soldiers live with. Except for the short periods of violent action, the battlefield is grim, empty and silent. The Chinese bugles and trumpets blowing at night only increased the soldiers' fear and anxiety, knowing that death could strike without warning, and that at any minute you could be in hand-to-hand combat with the enemy.

The 8th Army had been ordered to proceed north by General Douglas MacArthur, they had been met with overwhelming force, and now were unprepared to execute any kind of orderly withdrawal or retreat. After the battles at Kunuri, the 8th Army withdrawal south became a rout, not a retreat, and all because of the recklessness at the top; the refusal to heed the intelligence from the ground in Korea, and the stubbornness of General Douglas MacArthur and his staff of sycophants in Tokyo.

By November 30, five days after the Chinese attacks along the Chongchon River, the signals coming from General MacArthur had lost all of their previous optimism. MacArthur was now warning that the Chinese were planning for the total defeat of the United Nations forces, and the capture of the entire Korean peninsula. General Walker ordered the 8th Army to establish a new defensive line about 20 miles south of the Chongchon River where they planned to stand and fight. However, as the Chinese army came forward in such overwhelming numbers causing heavy American casualties, General Walker ordered his troops to again withdraw. He ordered the evacuation of the North Korean capital of Pyongyang, and the destruction of the huge stockpiles of equipment, ammunition and fuel. By December 5, 1950, huge fires were burning around the city and the bridges over the Taedong River were demolished. It is reported that more than 10,000 tons of ammunition, equipment, fuel, and supplies were set on fire that day.

As the American army withdrew in the face of the Chinese assault, the 8th Army had a few occasions when they were able to stop and regroup. During these times, when the Americans were not in battlefield contact with the enemy, the Chinese also halted their advance to allow their supplies and logistics to catch up with them. At this time, the morale among the American GIs was extremely low. The weather was very cold;

deep concern and fear of this unknown and formidable enemy was pervasive; and panic was beginning to set in among the troops. In Washington, D.C., the Pentagon was in turmoil over the collapse of morale among the American enlisted men and officers. The term used at that time to describe withdrawal or retreat was "Bug Out," as in head south, or head for the rear, and "Bug Out Fever" was spreading throughout the 8th Army. One symptom of the "Bug Out Blues" was the readiness of whole formations of United Nations forces to take to the road and head south at the mere sound of Chinese bugles or loudspeakers blasting away. Another failure on the battlefield was the complete lack of leadership at all levels. This lack of morale and failure of leadership changed to some degree when General Matthew Ridgway replaced General Walker as head of the 8th Army. General Ridgway set up "Ridgway's Rules" and attempted to restore morale and leadership. He realized that the 8th Army was now incapable of mounting a counter offensive, but he ordered all units to step up their patrols, and make aggressive contact with the enemy. Ridgway then set up a defensive line along the Imjin River, that came under attack by the Chinese on December 30. The Imjin River was frozen and the Chinese attacked across the river at a point where the Republic of Korea forces were deployed. According to military reports, the Chinese had carefully prepared for this attack and had trained and supplied their infantry well, so that they could withstand the freezing temperatures. The infantrymen were coated with oil and grease to help them withstand the sub-zero weather. The Chinese advance resulted in a withdrawal of United Nations forces through Seoul where they again attempted to regroup and set up a defensive line. However, the Chinese assault continued into January 1951, when they once again halted their offensive operations, and gave time to their support units to catch up with their front line formations. At that time, the front line that separated the Chinese/North Korean forces from the United Nations troops was located about 30 miles south of Seoul and extended from the port town of Samchok on the Sea of Japan, on the east coast of Korea, westward through Wonju, and then on to the port city of Pyongtaek on the Yellow Sea, on the west coast of the Korean peninsula.

During February 1951, as the situation on the battlefield was going from bad to worse, the United Nations was debating the Korean War, and voted on whether to brand China as an aggressor nation. This motion failed to pass, and the Chinese delegation claimed that the aggressor was the United Nations forces, especially the United States. Faced with the existing situation, the Truman administration and the Joint Chiefs of Staff were confronted with the following alternatives:

1. They could recommend reinforcement of United Nations troops, and attempt, once again, to advance northward to the Yalu River. The objective would be to impose a reunification of Korea by force.

2. The United Nations forces could withdraw completely from the Korean peninsula and hope for the best.

3. The United States could hold firm on the existing front lines and hold peace talks during the military stalemate.

4. An attempt could be made to obtain a cease fire agreement, followed by negotiations that would lead to a stalemate on the ground. The line separating the Chinese/North Koreans from the United Nations forces would be at the 38th parallel, the line as it existed before the North Korean invasion.

General MacArthur, the China Lobby in the United States, and their fellow hawks recommended Option # 1; Reunification of Korea, by force, using atomic weapons, if necessary. The Truman administration decided on Option 4; the stalemate/cease fire position, to be followed by negotiations and stalemate at the 38th parallel.

# *THE BATTLES AT KUNURI AND THE GAUNTLET*

After the attack by the Chinese army on November 26, the next several days were chaotic for the enlisted men of the 8th Army. The officers were trying to determine the best way out of their battlefield situation, but they were receiving no coherent orders from their command post. There was almost a complete lack of communication between units, but there was no lack of rumors regarding just about everything. Rumors about which roads south were opened or closed; rumors about the fanaticism of the Chinese forces; rumors about the overwhelming number of Chinese infantrymen; rumors about the Chinese burp gun and what an awesome weapon it was; rumors about reinforcements on their way to save the day; there were even rumors that the Chinese were about to surrender. The reality on the ground was the freezing temperatures, disoriented troops, and a division headquarters that was essentially paralyzed—not able to make a decision. The decision was finally made to head south down the Sunchon road, and the 8th Army survivors began their retreat from Kunuri on November 29, 1950.

When the Americans started their withdrawal they were exhausted and confused. The Chinese infantrymen seemed to be everywhere, and now they were reported to be within one mile of the 9th Regiment, 2nd Division headquarters. The Chinese did not have heavy weapons like the 105mm and 115 mm howitzers, but they had mortars and machine guns, and they were reportedly very good with these weapons. They were also very good with their so-called burp gun. Burp guns threw out a lot of firepower at close range, and, according to many American officers and enlisted men, the burp gun proved to be the best basic infantry weapon in Korea. It did not have the accuracy of the M-1 rifle or the carbine, but it amped up a lot more firepower, and much faster. In the close hand-to-hand combat conditions in Korea the burp gun proved to be a formidable weapon, and it outperformed and out-gunned the American weapons. The burp gun, according to many American infantrymen. sounded like a can of marbles when you shook them, (which may be why it was called a "Burp Gun") but on full automatic it sprayed a lot of bullets, and most of the killing in Korea was done at very close range and it was done quickly; survival was a matter of who reacted faster. In situations like that, the Chinese burp gun outgunned and outclassed what the Americans had. A close-in patrol fight was over very quickly, and usually the Americans lost because of this.

As the Chinese closed in they opened up with their mortars and machine guns, and then all hell broke loose. Another Chinese mortar attack followed and it was clear that the only way out for the Americans was to retreat down the road going south. The retreat had barely begun, when the road became littered with dead soldiers, disabled vehicles and masses of refugees fleeing their homes and heading south with their belongings on their backs. It was a chaotic situation for everyone as the American enlisted men were again forced to endure an unbelievable battlefield defeat, a battlefield that looked like a scene from Dante's "Inferno," except that in Korea at that time the temperatures were below freezing; it was an enlisted man's nightmare come front and center.

The road from Kunuri south to Sunchon had to pass through an area that would become known as the Gauntlet. This gauntlet area was several miles long, and the road was bordered on both sides by high mountain ridges. As the Americans headed into this area, the Chinese infantrymen, positioned on the ridges, opened up on the Americans from both sides of the roadway. It turned out that the Americans, in their withdrawal and on their officers orders, had marched right into one of the worst ambushes in United States military history.

It became apparent to the Americans immediately that getting through this pass could easily be stopped by the enemy by just setting up a roadblock. The Chinese did, in fact, set up roadblocks and the retreating American columns of GIs were forced to come to a standstill as the Chinese began firing on them from the high ground all around them. The United Nations troops and officers immediately realized that they had marched into an ambush that left them with few alternatives, none of them good. The Gauntlet was already littered with United Nations vehicles, and the overpowering noise from the battlefield caused by mortars, burp guns, and heavy weapons made the situation on the ground even worse.

During any withdrawal from a battlefield frontline, every officer and every enlisted man wants the withdrawal to be organized, and the objective should be getting to a defensible perimeter where the troops could regroup. In the days following the Chinese attack, however, the battlefield conditions turned into a soldier's nightmare, and got worse minute by minute. Add to this the fact that the military intelligence was minimal and erratic; radio communication was almost non-existent and what there was, was met with Chinese radio interference; the officers were confused and unable to issue realistic orders; no orders or commands were coming from General MacArthur and his advisors in Tokyo; food was limited to C-rations if the troops were lucky, and personal hygiene was non-existent; this all resulted in a complete breakdown and lack of morale among all the troops.

This was the situation on the ground as the Americans were heading south in withdrawal. They were also heading toward a potentially dangerous area in the Gauntlet that became know as "The Pass." The Pass was a section of the Gauntlet that would completely expose the troops to enemy fire. As the Americans moved through this area, as ordered, there was a complete breakdown of order and hierarchy due to a lack of leadership. When order and structure are lost in the Army, it is almost impossible to get it back, at least not until the battlefield situation changes for the better. What happened was a complete disintegration of an American division that was under attack from all sides by an overwhelming enemy force, and with no exit strategy available. For example, a vehicle would be hit, and cause a blocking of the roadway. Then, as some soldiers tried to move the vehicle off the road, the Chinese poured firepower down on them, and burp guns were firing from all around them. It was chaotic. Bodies were lying everywhere, many were dead but some were alive and calling for help. There were some medics in the area, but they had trouble assessing who was dead or who was badly wounded, or who was paralyzed and broken in spirit. The medics were working on the battlefield while under fire, and that made it impossible for them to render an assessment or offer proper care. The story of the battles along the Chongchon River and the Gauntlet, when the Chinese entered the war in November 1950, is described by military historian S.L.A. Marshall, in his book "The River and the Gauntlet." This is a description of the Chinese attack along the Chongchon River, and it is especially informative from an enlisted man's perspective.

From time to time, in this bleak battlefield situation, the officer or non-commissioned officer in charge, was able to form a mini-unit, and return fire in fast spasms of combat, but then the confusion in the group would return and cause them to disperse, and they would have to continue their withdrawal to what they hoped was relative safety, to the south and to the rear. Somehow, some of the survivors of the Chinese assault made it to Sunchon, a town about 50 miles south of Kunuri.

## *THE ARTILLERY DISASTER IN THE GAUNTLET*

As United Nations troops retreated from the Chongchon River in December 1950, there were huge problems for the retreating artillery battalions. The infantry was able to move more freely than the artillery, who were always held back by their big guns. The artillery, with their howitzers and unfavorable Korean terrain, had to move much more slowly, and was forced to become the division rearguard, having to repel enemy infantry that were attacking the rear of the American lines as they withdrew.

As darkness fell along the Gauntlet, the Americans were forced to "wait-in-line" as their troops slowly moved toward the Pass and went through it. To add to the chaos and confusion, the troops could see up ahead, the blazing tracer fire being poured down on the Americans from the Chinese who were hunkered down in the surrounding hills. On top of that were the American air strikes who were rushing to get in their final strikes before darkness closed down. And very often, these American bombing and strafing runs, because of darkness and pilot confusion as to who the enemy was, were raining down friendly fire on their own troops. In the early months of the Korean War, according to military reports, the American pilots often were not able to differentiate the enemy from the allied and ROK troops. Many of the pilots have reported that as they were flying overhead and getting ready to drop their ordnance, it was impossible to tell the North Korean soldiers from the South Korean and American troops.

The Americans ordered their Quad-50s to spray the hillsides where the enemy was dug in. The artillery was finally able to deploy their 155mm howitzers, and they began shelling the adjoining ridgelines.

These howitzers were often used during the first months of the war to fire point blank at the enemy infantry as they advanced on American lines. All along the Gauntlet, the American infantry and artillery were practically at a standstill, taking enemy fire as if they were sitting ducks in a shooting gallery. The commanding officers had to decide whether to stand their ground as they were on the roadway, and wait for a forward break-up through the Pass, or if they should form a perimeter consisting of the artillery and the remaining battalion, and try to last through the night. Fortunately for the officers, that decision did not have to be made, because the Pass began to clear and all units began a slow forward movement.

As the Americans proceeded through the Pass, they passed hundreds of burning and abandoned American vehicles. The roadway was littered with bedrolls, packs, destroyed jeeps, air mattresses, duffle bags and weapons. The road shoulders were also littered with dead Americans and other United Nations troops, and with the wounded who had managed to crawl to the side of the road but did not have the strength to get on their feet and join the withdrawal.

The ambush that the United Nations forces had to endure as they passed along the Gauntlet and through the Pass resulted in huge numbers of casualties. The hospitals in the zone past the Gauntlet and the Pass were overflowing with wounded, and many were lying on the ground outside the hospital in the freezing winter cold. It is reported that the physicians were working day and night, and were treating more than 600 cases each day.

The artillery units that were in the retreating column of United Nations forces suffered heavy equipment and gun losses. The artillery men also took very heavy casualties, and many had to fight as infantrymen as they fought off the enemy; and many of the survivors were awarded the Combat Infantry Badge and Silver Star for their battlefield heroism. It has been reported that these heavy artillery losses were due in large part to the mortal fear of the enemy, as well as to the extreme weather and terrain obstacles, and that gun losses were dependent upon the location of the battalion in the artillery column. Those in the front of the column went through with the largest number of howitzers saved, whereas those bringing up the rear lost more big guns, and found the roadway covered with rubble, wreckage, blocked roads and dead bodies.

If there was anyone to blame for the disastrous situation in Korea during the first year of the Korean War, a year when 400 to 500 Americans were being killed in action every week, it fell on those officers in Tokyo, officers that rarely, if ever, set foot in Korea; officers who were unable to admit that they had allowed their troops to blunder into a catastrophic trap set by the Chinese Army. The Chinese had even sent out strong warnings about what might happen if Allied forces pushed too close to the Manchurian border, including their statements to this effect at the United Nations. General Douglas MacArthur, whose refusal to heed these warnings at the U.N., and the warning battles at Unsan and Sudong, and then in defiance of intelligence about the size and intentions of the Chinese forces, ordered his troops to proceed north to the Yalu River, was responsible for one of the worst military defeats in United States military history.

MAC ARTHUR SAYS, YOU'VE GOT TO ATTACK
BUT YOU FOLLOW MAC AND YOU'LL NEVER COME BACK
WE'RE MOVING ON, WE'RE MOVING ON
YOU FOLLOW MAC AND YOU'LL NEVER COME BACK
WE'RE MOVING ON.

## *THE SHOOTOUT AT CHINAMEN'S HAT*

Along the southern border of the Chongchon River lies a range of high mountain-like ridges that are located between the villages of Kujong and Sinkung. As the United States forces were moving north in November 1950, one of the many problems they encountered was that of finding enough flat tracts of land to set up a perimeter and base their division artillery. This was a problem for the artillery in all Korean operations. Along the Chongchon River, on November 25 and 26, the rice paddies were iced over but not frozen solid, and the rest of the river valley was devoid of flat, barren spaces that are necessary for artillery operations. The hills overlapped each other, and the river beds were winding and uneven. In countryside terrain such as this, mortars are indispensable, but proper artillery placement is not possible.

However, there was a break in the landscape along the Chongchon River between Kujong and Sinkung that was perfectly flat. The draw was over 4,500 yards long and was capable of holding several battalions. This flat draw was just to the northwest of a mountain peak called Chinamen's Hat, so named because of its shape. Enemy forces were in possession of Chinamen's Hat and from their vantage point they could see every movement made by United States forces as they set up their perimeter and artillery. The Americans were able to establish cover in this flat area by using foxholes, bunkers, and trenches that had been left from earlier military operations. At this point, the Chinese had not officially entered the war, so although the United Nations forces were on the alert, they felt confident of their position, artillery placement, and relative safety.

Then at about 7 pm, as it was getting dark, some of the men in their foxholes said they heard rifle fire in the distance. The rifle fire was followed by the eerie sound of bugles and trumpets blowing. Not long after the sound of the bugles, more than seven columns of Chinese infantrymen crossed the Chongchon River and swarmed right into the American position.

The Americans were not familiar with the bizarre fighting tactics of the enemy. They were also late in setting up camp and many were exhausted; this, followed by the timing of the Chinese strike that coincided with that period of dusk when vision is most impaired, resulted in complete disorientation among the Americans. All of these factors, plus the false optimism of the officers as evidenced by the faulty intelligence estimates of the enemy capabilities, all factored into the total surprise of the Chinese attack. The Chinese came on in waves, and then more waves of enemy infantry followed; the large numbers of the Chinese and the suddenness of the attack overwhelmed the Americans. The survivors of the initial attack headed for the rear, and they were closely followed by Chinese infantrymen. As the men retreated they were joined by forces in the rear where they attempted to set up a secondary defense line. These secondary defensive lines, however, were overrun almost immediately by more waves of Chinese infantry, so that soon the Americans were in full flight toward the rear. As they ran they were yelling "I'm a GI—GI" and "I'm American—I'm American," hoping that they would not be shot by friendly fire as they retreated. It was total chaos.

The Americans finally reached high ground and were able to hold their position. However, the Chinese still maintained their hold on Chinamen's Hat despite heavy mortar and machine gun fire; yet the price they paid in manpower was considerable. It is reported that more than 400 Chinese died in the fighting, and at least 100 were taken prisoner. The Americans reportedly lost 200 killed and wounded.

What happened at Chinamen's Hat was not, at that time, given the strategic significance that it deserved. Military analysts, at that time, said it was an isolated battle, unrelated to any strategic enemy planning. However, it is now known that this was an unsupported and dangerous conclusion to make regarding the affair at "The Hat." The military now believe that when the encounter at Chinamen's Hat is viewed in prospective, and assessed with all the other strikes that the Chinese made all along the Chongchon River that day, that their attack across the river at Chinamen's Hat was part of a battlefield strategy that was put in full operation when the Chinese entered the war in late November 1950.

# CHOSIN RESEVOIR: NOVEMBER-DECEMBER, 1950

In the middle of November 1950, the X Corps Marines landed at Wonson, a port town on the eastern coast of the Korean peninsula, about 100 miles north of the 38$^{th}$ parallel. As the Marines moved north toward the Chosin Reservoir, many in command positions were warning of potential disaster ahead. They warned of the threat of being lured by the enemy into the mountains, and then cut off from the coast, stopping a possible retreat, and then being wiped out in the frozen, bleak mountains in Korea.

Major General O.P. Smith, commander of the 1$^{st}$ Marines, X Corps, was operating in the eastern area of Korea in the vicinity of Wonsan. It was November 27 and the Marines were headed north toward the Chosin Reservoir, an area near the Yalu River and the Manchurian border. General Smith, distrustful of General MacArthur's orders to advance toward Manchuria, felt that the Chinese were laying a trap for the Americans, as his Marines headed over the bridge at Funchilin Pass, about 30 miles south of the Chosin Reservoir. The Chinese had not blown the bridge at Funchilin Pass and General Smith felt sure they had not demolished the bridge on purpose, so that the Americans could easily cross over into a Chinese ambush.

The Funchilin Pass was a narrow chasm with an impassable cliff on one side and a sharp valley on the other, and United States intelligence told General Smith that the Chinese had at least six divisions in the area. In order for the Americans to proceed north they would have to pass over a concrete bridge that covered several gigantic pipes; pipes that pumped water from the Chosin Reservoir to a nearby power plant.

General Smith knew that if the Chinese demolished that bridge, it would mean the end of the American offensive advance to the north. The fact that the Chinese left the bridge intact, meant to General Smith that the Chinese wanted the Americans to cross it, thus isolating themselves, and opening the United Nations forces for a devastating attack. Regardless of the situation on the ground, and despite the intelligence warning that Chinese forces were massing north of the Chosin Reservoir and along the Yalu River, the orders from MacArthur were to advance northward.

A staff officer for General Almond of the X Corps, referred to MacArthur's strategic planning, before and after the Chinese entered the war, "as plans that bore no resemblance to the country in which we were fighting. It was like complete insanity in the command." He went on to state, "From the time we headed for the Yalu River it was like being in the nut house, with the nuts in charge. You could only understand the totality of the madness if you were up there in the north after the Chinese had entered in full force, and we were being hit and hit again by these immense numbers of troops. The only real question was whether we could get any of our people out of there—and yet the orders from Tokyo were still to go forward." Then he added that "MacArthur, after Inchon, was nutty as a fruitcake."

On November 27, 1950, the enemy was attacking from all sides, and because of the extreme cold the Americans had trouble firing their Browning automatic rifles (BARs), that now would only fire single rounds. Then at night on November 28, the Americans prepared for another onslaught. The Chinese made probing attacks and then withdrew and remained silent. Occasionally, whistles would blow and loudspeakers would blare out messages addressing the troops; telling the Americans that, "Tonight GI, lay down arms, surrender," followed by, "Tonight, Americans, you die."

After dark on the 28th of November, the Chinese again probed the American defenses, and then with bugles blowing the Chinese infantrymen began an overwhelming onslaught. The effects of fatigue and freezing weather was demoralizing the United States forces, and signs of panic began to spread among the troops and officers. When the order was given to withdraw, instead of leaving their emplacements and foxholes silently and undercover, whole platoons of Americans appeared at check points as they moved toward the rear, some without weapons or equipment. This alerted the Chinese who then renewed their attack. The retreating Americans moved down the road, and at times had to cross frozen ponds and lakes; the ice sometimes cracking and then giving away to swallow up the men from above; many of them drowning or freezing in the sub zero water. The surviving men dug in as best they could in the icy ground, an almost impossible task not only because of the frozen ground but also because many of them had thrown away their entrenching tools. The artillery by then was down to a few big guns, the rest having gotten bogged down in the terrain, overrun or captured. That night the men were cramped into a narrow defensive perimeter. It was desperately cold and even the men who still had their sleeping bags were afraid to go to sleep for fear of freezing to death, or being bayoneted while they slept. Also, in order to prevent their weapons from freezing up they had to be fired every 15 to 20 minutes.

On the following afternoon, the 29th of November, the United States Air Force air dropped supplies and ammunition, that was followed by air strikes against the enemy during which bombs and napalm were dropped to great effect. However, the Chinese attack continued and the enemy was able to infiltrate into the American rifle companies. The commander ordered the survivors to withdraw and head south to Hagaru where the Marines were still holding out. The Americans withdrew, but many of them were disoriented, not knowing which way to go, as they wandered aimlessly across frozen lakes and rice paddies. Looking back on the villages they had just left, the American soldiers could see that the buildings and homes in the villages were burning, as the Chinese foraged through the rubble looking for survivors.

The wounded survivors of the X Corps Marines were cared for at the garrison medical unit at Hagaru, a town about ten miles southeast of the Chosin Reservoir. The marines then received orders to destroy all remaining heavy equipment, and leave behind their weapons and vehicles, and head south toward Sudong, a village about 50 miles west of the port city of Hungnam. The military reported that the although the marines were retreating, they did so in the highest tradition of the Marine Corps.

By December 6, the Marines were moving southeast along the road to Hungnam and the coast. The final march to the sea was interrupted frequently by Chinese ambushes; and bridges and overpasses had been blown up by Chinese infiltrators and North Korean soldiers. To make matters worse, the roads were jammed by masses of civilian refugees that were trailing along behind the retreating Americans. Finally, at a town near Sudong, trains and trucks were waiting to take the men to the relative safety of Hungnam. During the U.S. evacuation, the Chinese were held off by the combined air power of the U.S. Marines and Navy, while the 7th Fleet stood offshore giving massive big gun support, including the 16 inch guns of the U.S.S. Missouri.

By December 15, the Marines had been taken off the Korean peninsula, and they were followed by the Republic of Korea forces. The evacuation of troops and civilian personnel also included taking more than 85,000 refugees safely to sea. The ships of the 7th Fleet then took the troops, civilian personnel, and refugees back to Japan. As the last ships hauled out to sea, the port of Hungnam was blown up and destroyed. All rail lines were destroyed and large quantities of fuel and explosives were set on fire.

If there was anything symbolic or tragic that demonstrated the disconnect between MacArthur's Tokyo headquarters and the battlefield, it was the bizarre orders that were issued from Tokyo in the midst of the crises. These orders had no relation with the situation on the ground at either Kunuri along the Chongchon River in the west, or at the Chosin Reservoir on the eastern battlefield. When orders finally came from Tokyo to pull back, it was already too late. It was too late for the American infantrymen, many of whom had already been killed in action, and the delay in issuing orders had resulted in heavy casualties and loss of equipment and ammunition. The survivors had already started heading for the rear, where further attacks from the Chinese awaited them along the Funchilin Pass. The delay from Tokyo in ordering a withdrawal of troops only benefited the Chinese army, as it gave them time to re-supply and to organize their ambush battle plans at the Funchilin Pass.

# *THE REACTION OF WASHINGTON, D.C. AND GENERAL MACARTHUR TO THE CHINESE ENTRY INTO THE KOREAN WAR*

In the days following the Chinese attack, and as it became clear that the Americans were suffering a disastrous defeat, the stark contrast between the reality on the ground in Korea and the confident statements coming from General MacArthur and his advisors back in Tokyo was absolute. The Tokyo press briefings conducted by MacArthur's staff, insisted that the General had been right all along, that their intelligence on the Chinese was correct, and the briefing officer seemed unshaken by any reports about defeat from the battlefield. When one of the reporters asked why General MacArthur ordered his troops northward when he knew that the Chinese had at least 30 infantry divisions along the Yalu River in striking distance of American forces, the briefing officer reportedly replied that we couldn't just passively sit by. We had to attack and find out the enemy profile. It was reasoning such as this that led to the disastrous battles along the Chongchon River and at the Chosin Reservoir in late November 1950. The young men on the ground in Korea at that time, many of them with no combat training, had no idea about the size and strength of the Chinese forces as they followed MacArthur's orders and headed toward the Manchurian border. They still believed what MacArthur had told them in his now famous home-by Christmas pledges, pledges that had nothing to do with the reality on the ground and MacArthur's own intelligence. Knowing what he did, General MacArthur blithely sent these young Americans forward into what was to become a disastrous and bloody defeat for these young GIs. An officer in the Tokyo office of General MacArthur is reported to have said that MacArthur refused to acknowledge the situation on the ground in Korea. He was trying to run the war from 700 miles away, in the safety of his offices in Tokyo. It's madness, pure madness!! Someone is crazy. Those GIs were, in fact, marched into a battlefield disaster from which few of them returned, and General MacArthur was never held accountable for the military decisions he made at that time.

The MacArthur office in Tokyo was quick to place the blame for everything that was happening in Korea, on Washington D.C., the Truman administration, and the Joint Chiefs of Staff. They claimed that Washington and the Pentagon had hamstrung MacArthur, and prevented him from bombing Chinese bases in Manchuria and along the Yalu River. General MacArthur published articles in American newspapers that were in agreement with his battlefield strategy, in which he stated that "not allowing his $8^{th}$ Army to go in hot pursuit of the Chinese and to bomb their Manchurian bases had placed him with an enormous military handicap."

In Washington, the Truman administration, having thought that the war was virtually over in November, was now faced with a military disaster and a commanding general who was presenting himself as the administration's most serious critic, militarily and politically. The reports to Washington and the Pentagon from General MacArthur were now highly pessimistic. Whereas before the Chinese attack he was supremely confident, always underestimating the Chinese threat, now, after the Chinese entry into the war, he was intent on exaggerating everything. MacArthur now claimed that he faced more than 500,000 Chinese infantrymen on the battlefield, and that his airpower was completely impotent because he was not allowed to bomb the Chinese Manchurian bases, possibly employing atomic weapons.

The fact that the Truman administration seemed unable to make important decisions angered General Matthew Ridgway, then a senior officer at the Pentagon. Ridgway had always disagreed with MacArthur's northward offensive after the success at Inchon, as he believed that it put the American infantrymen at too great a risk. He saw the situation developing in Korea as one with no clear strategy, with very little thought to the possible consequences. Now, as the battlefield was collapsing around the Americans, Ridgway was appalled at MacArthur's failure to act and get in control; he was also alarmed by the Truman administration's lack of command and their inability to take charge. However, General Ridgway never confronted MacArthur about his decision to advance northward.

In the meantime, General MacArthur's 8th Army and X Corps were in full-scale retreat. The phrase "The Great Bugout" came out during the American withdrawal, and the Pentagon and military analysts began placing the blame for this military collapse on everyone except their own leadership. Military historians are still attempting to place the blame for the American withdrawal on the fighting units of the Republic of Korea army; some of these historians have even attempted to place the blame on some segregated African-American units. These racist statements can only have come from military officers, probably educated at West Point and who never served in an actual combat zone, and who made these claims without any first hand combat experience in Korea. The reality on the ground was that everyone was in full retreat at that time, and the fault for this disaster should be placed right at the feet of the military leadership. The American retreat covered approximately 120 miles in two weeks, when the Chinese army finally relented. By the time the battlefield had cleared in January 1951, the Americans were back to a line about 30 miles south of the 38th parallel. The front line extended from the port city of Samchok on the east coast of Korea, westward through Wonju in the Central Corridor, and then to the town of Pyongtaek on the west coast, a front line located essentially in the same area as when the war had started just seven months before.

# KOREA
## LINES OF ADVANCE, 1950-1951

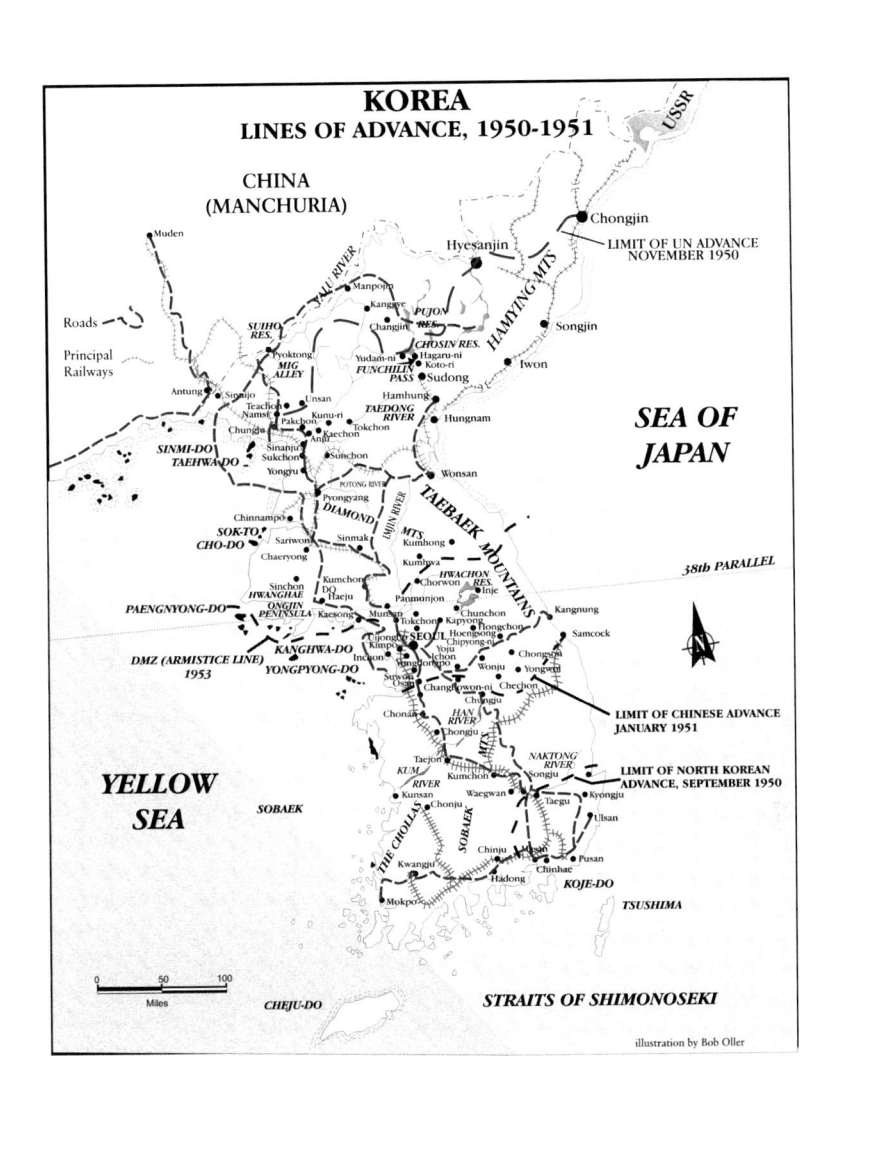

*illustration by Bob Oller*

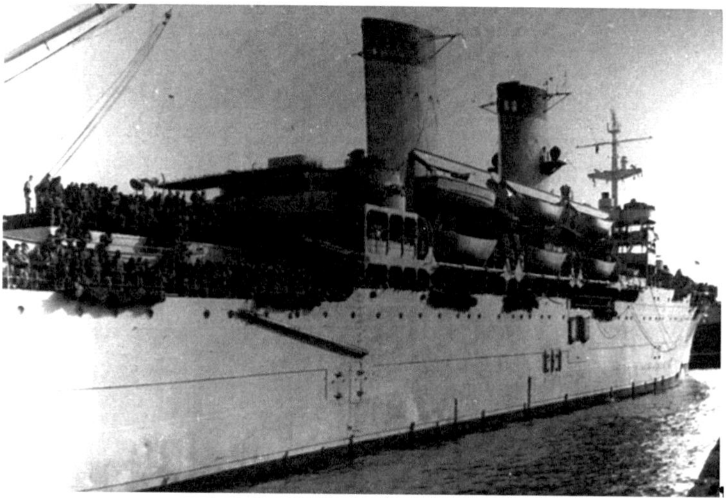

*The conditions on the troop ships during the Korean War were extremely crowded. The rough weather and rocking decks made life miserable for soldiers, many of whom were seasick for the entire crossing.*

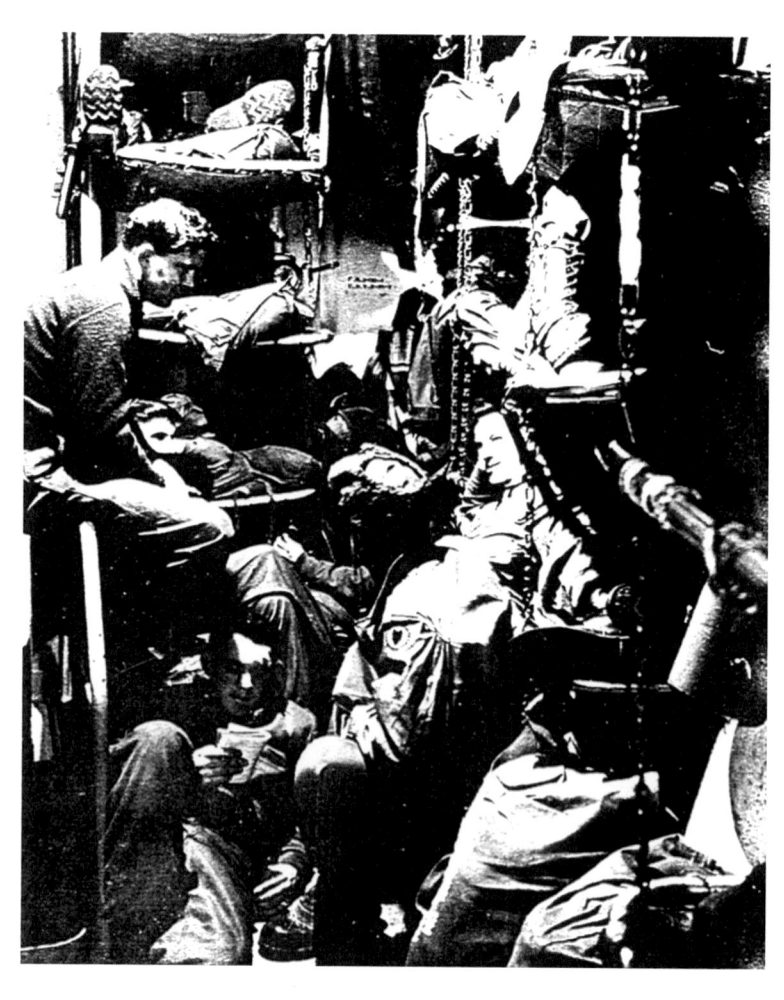

*The enlisted men headed for Korea in 1950 were jammed into half-lit, unventilated, compartments deep in the ship's holds. The bunks were stacked up six to eight deep and the men had to share their bunk with their 50 pound duffle bag and M-1 rifle. The trip from California to Japan lasted 30 days and some of these men did not survive the trip across the Pacific Ocean.*

*During the rainy season in Korea, the G.I.s had to dig deep trenches around their pup tents to keep their equipment and weapons from being washed away in the flooding rainfall. When the men dug their foxholes, they were half full of water before they finished digging*

7.62mm Type 50 Chinese Submachine Gun (Chinese Burp Gun)

illustration by Bob Oller

The Chinese burp gun was a Soviet made submachine gun. It weighed 8 pounds and fired at the rate of 900 rounds per minute. The burp gun threw out a lot of fire power, and according to many American officers and enlisted men, the burp gun was the most effective basic infantry weapon used in the Korean War. It did not have the accuracy of the M1 rifle or the carbine, but it carried a lot more fire power, and was much faster. In the close range combat conditions in Korea, "the Chinese burp gun out-classed and out-gunned the weapons we had," according to General Hal Moore. "A close in patrol fight was over very quickly, and because of the burp gun we lost many of those battles."

*Radio operators and* BAR *men were prime targets for the North Korean and Chinese infantrymen and snipers.*

*This is the site of the battle of Heartbreak Ridge which was a continuation of the fight at Bloody Ridge. The battles were ferocious with both sides fighting to a virtual stalemate, as hundreds of American enlisted men were killed in action. This desolated ridge is a good example of the non-strategic Korean terrain where many battles took place from 1951 to 1953. The Korean War ground on as the American G.I. fought trench warfare, hand-to-hand combat with fixed bayonets, and endured constant artillery and mortar barrages as combat fatigue spread among the troops. There was almost no meaning whatever to the fighting and dying.*

## The M1 / Garand

illustration by Bob Oller

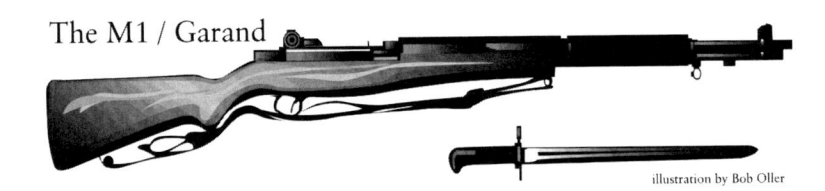

*A semi-automatic rifle, gas operated; loads an eight-round .30-caliber clip, and weighs 9.5 pounds.*

The Carbine .30 caliber

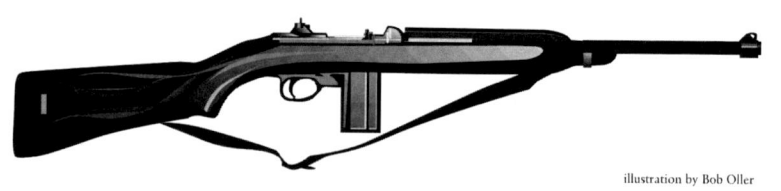

illustration by Bob Oller

*A full automatic weapon that fires a .30 caliber bullet, and weighs 6 pounds. The carbine has far less range than the M1 rifle with less stopping power.*

Browning Automatic Rifle (BAR)

illustration by Bob Oller

*A full automatic weapon that can be operated one shot at a time. When on full automatic the BAR will put out up to 500 .30 caliber rounds per minute. The BAR weighs 16 pounds and may be fired from the hip, shoulder or bipod.*

## Infantry Mortars

illustration by Bob Oller

    The mortar is a simple sealed-breech tube supported by a base plate, and comes in three sizes: 60-mm, 81-mm, and 4.2 inch. The mortar is useful for lobbing shells at a high angle at targets that are protected by hills, ridge lines or some other obstacle. The projectile is dropped into the muzzle of the mortar and has a range up to 4,000 yards.

## 3.5 Bazooka

illustration by Bob Oller

*The inside diameter of the launcher is 3.5 inches. The bazooka fires an 8.5 pound rocket which contains a hollow shaped charge that can be concentrated on a small area or target. The large rocket has a maximum range of several hundred yards, but to be effective against medium tanks the bazooka should be within 70 yards or less of the target. The 3.5 bazooka is usually handled by a two-man team.*

## Wheeled Vehicle Mounted With Quad-50

illustration by Bob Oller

*The Quad-50 is a vehicle with four mounted .50 caliber Browning machine guns. These weapons may be fired singly or as a unit. In Korea, the Quad-50s were a main support of the infantry line. The battery fire of the Quad-50 is overpowering and brackets the target. For the enemy caught in the fire of a Quad-50 there seems to be no escape and it was the No. 1 demoralizer of enemy infantry in Korea.*

## *GENERAL MATHEW RIDGWAY REPLACES GENERAL WALKER*

General Walton Walker, commander of the 8$^{th}$ Army during the first months of the Korean War, led his forces from the Pusan Perimeter north past the 38$^{th}$ parallel and, on orders from General MacArthur, on toward the Yalu River. It is reported that when he visited his 8$^{th}$ Army units he declined helicopter transportation and always went by jeep. General Walker and his driver were known to have always driven fast and sometimes recklessly, and that he and his driver often pushed their jeep too fast on the narrow, icy roads in Korea. These Korean roads, during the first year of the war, were also badly stacked up with troops advancing and retreating, with refugees fleeing their homes and the violence, and with abandoned army vehicles that closed off the roads. It was a traffic nightmare for civilians and the military. On the morning of December 23, 1950, General Walton Walker and his driver, an aide and a bodyguard were speeding north when a South Korean weapons carrier swung out into his lane. Walker's driver tried to avoid a collision, but the jeep flipped over and all four men were thrown into the ditch. General Walker was killed almost immediately as he sustained life ending injuries, while the other three survived. At the time of Walker's death he was reported to have been exhausted and "beaten down" because of his campaign from Pusan to North Korea. He felt that General MacArthur was about to relieve him from command as he was not in agreement with MacArthur's campaign strategy to head north and challenge the Chinese. As it turned out, General Walker, because of his death, would not be remembered for his valiant, even heroic efforts at the Pusan Perimeter, and his push to the 38$^{th}$ parallel after the Inchon landing. Ironically, his epitaph would be the disastrous battles that took place up along the Yalu River; battles that he believed were ill conceived, at best, and outright dangerous with no clear objectives, at worst. Unfortunately, his beliefs and concerns would turn out to be proven correct as the war progressed. However, General Walker received his fourth star, posthumously, and he received high praise from MacArthur; but his accidental death was an inglorious way to end a distinguished career.

General Walker was replaced by General Matthew Bunker Ridgway at a time when the 8th Army was on the verge of defeat. The 8th Army had suffered major military defeats at the hands of the Chinese Army along the banks of the Chongchon River in North Korea, and had to retreat back to the 38th parallel. The troops were demoralized and ready to call it quits; they wanted to get out of what they saw as a god-forsaken country, a no-man's land. The slogan heard frequently from the men on the ground was, "die for a tie." Although MacArthur saw a stalemate as a humiliating defeat, his troops saw a stalemate on the battlefield as a way out. General Ridgway had none of the vainglorious grandiosity of MacArthur, although he is reported to have had his own strict purpose—a certain mystique and a personal and lofty sense of his role in history. He is reported to have been fiercely aggressive, unsparing of himself, and demanding of those under his command; and he is reported to have been relatively humorless. He became known to the troops under him soon after he took command, by showing up close to the front line (although always well back of Danger Rear), to "talk" with the troops. He was always decked out in well pressed battle fatigues, well shined combat boots, and his trademark hand grenades dangling from his shoulders and belt; hand grenades he was not planning to use, and that he had probably never thrown except when he took his officer's basic training course back in the States. The troops had also heard that General Ridgway was at least as aggressive as MacArthur, and the men felt that is was easy for an officer to be aggressive, especially when they were well back of Danger Rear when they issued the orders, and when his aggressive tactics always directly affected the troops he commanded, and not the officers issuing the commands.

However, although General Ridgway was aggressive, it turned out that he also accepted the fact that the Truman administration was running the war, and trying to prevent an outbreak of war in Europe, where the Russians had recently placed so many armored divisions. The troops on the line heard many rumors about Ridgway, many stating that he was not as reckless as MacArthur. They also heard that he believed in the "Basics of Battle": that the infantry should get out on patrol; and that they should be fearless and aggressive. He is quoted as saying that "all lives on the battlefield are equal, and a dead soldier or a dead rifleman is as great a loss in the eyes of God as a dead general." However magnanimous this statement may have sounded, General Ridgway didn't comment on the fact that dead riflemen outnumber dead generals exponentially. And as it would eventually be shown in the future course of the Korean War, many thousands of 8th Army infantry and other soldiers would die under the command of the fearless, grenade carrying General Matthew Bunker Ridgway, as he and future generals leading the 8th Army, planned and carried out battles from the safety of their command posts in Danger Rear or Tokyo, and sent their men into combat, long after peace talks had started in Kaesong, Korea in July 1951.

General Ridgway arrived in Korea on December 26, 1950. He had been told by General MacArthur that the 8th Army was "his to command." On his arrival, Ridgway began to tour the forward positions where he found that morale was extremely low; there was a defeatist attitude among the officers and men; radio and Morse code communication was almost non-existent; and there was almost no military intelligence. Most front line units had no idea how many Chinese divisions were near them, and Ridgway immediately felt that this was because they were not sending out enough patrols. After his visits to forward line units, Ridgway is reported to have been extremely upset at the broken spirit of the men on the front line; he stated that the 8th Army "had not been in retreat, they were in full flight." He felt that the commanders in the field were too old to command, and out of touch and ill prepared for the war. The commanders who General Ridgway was complaining about, however, had been through five months of a war that none of them had been prepared for. Many of them were recent replacements into units of the 8$^{th}$ Army that had been overrun by a Chinese army of overwhelming force and numbers. There is no doubt that many of the commanders and all of the infantrymen were demoralized; however, they had good reason to be demoralized, and here was a general, fresh from the United States and Tokyo, who had not experienced what they had been through, talking to them as if they were in basic training. General Ridgway believed that you must be ruthless with your command officers because the army depends on their leadership.

General Ridgway, as most officers assuming new command do, laid down his own rules for proceeding; they were called the Ridgway Rules, and he soon became known as a feared "hard ass" who demanded results. He demanded that the most forward units get out on patrol and find the enemy. They were to "go on patrol, patrol, patrol." General Ridgway is reported to have said, "Nothing but your love of comfort, keeps you to the roads. You should get off the roads, find the enemy, and fix his position. Find them! Fix them! Fight them! Finish them!"

GENERAL RIDGWAY SAYS YOU CAN'T RETREAT
BUT YOU DON'T RETREAT, YOU'RE GONNA GET BEAT
WE'RE MOVING ON, WE'RE MOVING ON
CHINESE TRUMPETS BLOW, WE'VE GOT TO GO
WE'RE MOVING ON.

General Ridgway, now in charge in Korea, planned to keep MacArthur informed, but he did not fear MacArthur as other General officers did. Ridgway also had leverage with the Joint Chiefs of Staff in Washington, and he received all the personnel and equipment that he requested. Although General Ridgway was the new man in Korea, MacArthur was still the man in Tokyo calling the shots, who still controlled the overall strategy; so although Ridgway shared Washington's view of Korea as a limited war, this vision was not shared by General Douglas MacArthur and his circle of advisors in Tokyo.

# *GENERAL RIDGWAY'S BATTLES: CHIPYONGNU, TWIN TUNNELS, WONJU*

By early February 1951, the American and Chinese armies confronted one another once again. This time the confrontation was in an area of Korea known as the Central Corridor. This section of Korea is mountainous, and especially difficult for the American artillery to set up, and this favored the Chinese. The Chinese plan was to maintain their position along the Central Corridor, and their objective was to control the Chipyongnu-Wonju communication centers; this area was also an important rail terminal and road center connecting all parts of Korea and would become a fiercely contested battleground. The Americans knew that if the Chinese controlled this area, they would have a strong base from which to advance on Taegu, an important city about 100 miles south of Wonju. General Ridgway knew that if the Chinese won the battles of Chipyongnu and Wonju they would have an open corridor to Taegu and from there to Pusan. Military historians now know, however, that the Chinese battle strategy did not include advancing on Pusan or attempting to unify the country. The Chinese plan was to reach a stalemate in the vicinity of the 38th parallel, and then let the peace talks run their course. Both sides wanted to hold the terrain they had, and to fight only minor strategic battles to strengthen their respective positions at the peace talks. Based on these facts, General Ridgway ordered the 8th Army to stand and fight for the Central Corridor.

On February 12, 1951, United States infantry were digging in, as well as they could, in the frozen ground on the hills surrounding Chipyongnu. The Americans knew that the Chinese were massing several infantry divisions north of this area in what looked like preparation for an assault.

The Americans were preparing for the worst by laying barbed wire and land mines around their positions. They were being supplied by U.S. Air Force airdrops of weapons, ammunition and food supplies.

During the night of February 12, the Chinese bugles started blowing. Then the Chinese attacked, supported by mortar and machine gun fire, and started to move on the defensive perimeter of American forces. The Americans, greatly outnumbered, began making plans to withdraw. However, the 8th Army received orders from General Ridgway that Chipyongnu and Wonju should be defended and held at all cost. Ridgway told his commanders on the ground that if their units were surrounded they were to fight and hold their ground, and he ordered airdrops of ammunition and weapons to supply them so that they could counterattack. He also told his ground commanders that reinforcements were advancing from the south to provide support.

Then on February 13, the Chinese again began blowing bugles and whistles, and the loudspeakers were blaring out messages in English; all designed to spread panic among the American soldiers. The Chinese forces then began shelling the American perimeter with artillery and mortar fire. The battle continued for two days and the situation on the ground was tenuous. General Ridgway gave the 8th Army troops in these battles the highest priority for air support, and during February 14, 15 and 16 the Air Force conducted continuous bombing raids, dropping bombs and napalm. The Americans were able to hold their ground and counterattack and, supported by Marine and Air Force planes, they gave back to the enemy more firepower than they received, and held out until the American tank column of reinforcements arrived from the south.

Meanwhile, several other battles were raging around the village of Chipyongnu. The Americans, in these other battles, were under constant attack as the Chinese sought to maintain control of this strategic area. The American commander in these battles also called for air strikes, and a special task force was called in that included tanks, three infantry battalions, and artillery. The combination of air power, napalm, and artillery overwhelmed the Chinese infantrymen, and they were soon forced to withdraw.

## THE KOREAN PIPELINE

The armored column from the south that was sent to relieve the Americans at Chipyongnu was called Task Force Crombez, named after its commander Colonel Marcel Crombez. Task Force Crombez was made up of a company of tanks, backed up by three infantry battalions, and artillery. In order to reach Chipyongnu and provide the much needed support to the United Nations forces there, Task Force Crombez had to fight their way north through a series of Chinese ambushes. They arrived in time to stabilize the American position, and then to stage a counterattack. The combination of air power, the stand made by the 8th Army infantry, and the presence of Task Force Crombez stopped the Chinese and forced them to withdraw. It was seen as a success for the Americans, one of their few battlefield successes during the first year of the Korean War. However, the casualty report for the fighting around Chipyongnu included more than 50 killed in action, 250 wounded, and 42 missing in action. The Communist casualties were listed at more than 2,000 killed in action and 3,000 wounded.

Although no one realized it at the time, the battles around Chipyongnu and Wonju were a turning point for the Americans in the Korean War. Both battles were hard fought with both sides suffering heavy casualties, and it was especially difficult around Wonju. In the first part of the Wonju battle the Americans were hit so hard that the area became known as Massacre Valley. One soldier posted a large sign in the area that summed up the bitterness that the soldiers in Korea felt about the type of war the politicians were telling the American people about:

"MASSACRE VALLEY/SCENE OF HARRY TRUMAN'S POLICE ACTION/NICE GOING, HARRY."

The American and United Nations forces, however, held their line and caused the Chinese to relent and then withdraw. Although the battle at Wonju was tenuous at the beginning it turned out to be a victory in the end, and it was these battles at Chipyongnu and Wonju that would become the model for the Americans to follow in future battles with the formidable Chinese enemy. Military analysts now believe that these battles around Chipyongnu and Wonju gave the Americans renewed confidence; the United Nations forces had found their form, and despite times of crises in the months ahead, the 8$^{th}$ Army would never look back again.

There are American and British historians, however, who believe that the Chinese now felt that they had achieved their objective by driving the Americans away from Manchuria and south to the 38$^{th}$ parallel. These historians believe that the Chinese, after securing a line along the 38$^{th}$ parallel, had no intention of attempting to move into South Korea to unify the peninsula under Communist control.

Regardless of the intentions of both armies, it is clear that because of these battles and the success achieved by the Americans, the U.S. troops had re-gained their confidence and they had returned to fighting form.

## THE TWIN TUNNELS

The Twin Tunnels were located about three miles southeast of Chipyongnu. These tunnels channeled rail lines out in all directions across Korea's Central Corridor and the terrain in the tunnels area consisted of steep ridgelines, with a road running north and south. As the road heads north out of the valley it crosses the east-west railroad line between the two tunnels, that gave the area its name. One month after General Ridgway assumed command of the 8th Army, he began planning offensive operations, and his first major offensive involved the Twin Tunnels and was named Operation Thunderbolt; it was General Ridgway's attempt to gain initiative in the war.

There were three stages to the battle at the Twin Tunnels. The first stage was a reconnaissance patrol followed by two violent battles. The recon company was a relatively small force of four officers and 56 enlisted men. They had eight BARs, two heavy machine guns, a rocket launcher, a 60mm mortar, and two recoilless rifles. There was heavy snow, icy roads and heavy fog that made their advance slow and treacherous. The company reached the Twin Tunnels around noon where they were met by a sizable force of Chinese infantry. The American recon company fought off the Chinese, forcing them to withdraw, and then radioed their observations back to their Command Post.

After the reconnaissance was completed, the second stage of the offensive began, called Operation Roundup. The objective of Operation Roundup was to keep both Chipyongnu and Wonju from falling into Chinese hands. Not far from the tunnels, the Chinese attacked, hitting the Americans hard. The stage was now set for two major battles, battles in which the Americans were greatly outnumbered.

   These battles were hard fought with both sides suffering heavy casualties, testing the strength and resolve of both armies. Time and again the Chinese seemed ready to overrun the American position, but the Americans stood firm, shifting their troops and their position constantly until they gained control of the battlefield. Then the Americans staged a counterattack, firing every weapon they had, and charging the Chinese position with fixed bayonets. The intensity of the American counterattack finally broke the Chinese resolve and they began to retreat. Another factor in the Chinese retreat was the heavy air support that the Air Force provided. The American pilots dropped 500 pound bombs, called daisy cutters, right on top of where the Chinese were preparing a counterattack, essentially wiping them out. These bombs were followed by rockets called "gook goosers" by the troops, and these were backed up with 50 caliber machine guns. When the smoke cleared, the Chinese retreat continued and the battles were over, battles that would turn out to be a turning point for the Americans in the conduct of the Korean War.

## *GENERAL MACARTHUR, GENERAL RIDGWAY AND OPERATION KILLER*

After General Ridgway's successes at Chipyongnu and Wonju, General MacArthur developed a distrust and resentment toward General Ridgway. Matthew Ridgway had a blunt and candid style that appealed to the press corps, and MacArthur began to realize that the limelight, which he craved, was shifting away from him toward his subordinate. The press felt that General Ridgway was both professional and straight—a general concerned about his mission, and he spoke to reporters in an honest, blunt manner. There was a subtle tone that was emerging in press relations that MacArthur was not able to deal with; that is, there was an implicit sense that General Ridgway was now the positive beacon for the future, and he was replacing the out-of-touch General MacArthur, who had been trying to run a war from his offices back in Tokyo, several hundred miles from the battlefields in Korea.

When General Ridgway's Operation Killer was about to begin, General MacArthur flew to Korea, a trip he had only made once before, and he announced that it was he, MacArthur, who had planned and ordered Operation Killer. General MacArthur was not able to deal with the battlefield successes of his subordinate and he continually attempted to undermine Ridgway's authority and diminish his battlefield success.

General MacArthur's strategy had always been aggressive, and during wartime that is the preferred strategy. However, the Korean War posed battlefield conditions that had international ramifications that went far beyond the borders of Korea. MacArthur continually complained that the Truman Administration imposed limitations upon his command; he felt that they did not supply him with enough troops to get the job done;

and he complained the United States offered sanctuaries in Manchuria to the Chinese from American bombing attacks. However, General MacArthur and his friends in the China Lobby in the United States Congress, made no mention of the sanctuaries that the Americans had, most notably the industrial and port facilities of Yokahama and Tokyo, targets that were certainly within easy reach of the Chinese; targets that they did not attempt to target for bombing attacks. General MacArthur insisted on charging that the Truman Administration and the Joint Chiefs of Staff were unwilling to seek real victory, although he was not able to describe what real victory meant. General MacArthur always felt that a wider war with China and perhaps Russia, with the possible use of atomic weapons would lead to eventual victory for the United States, and the defeat of global Communism.

## *PRESIDENT TRUMAN AND THE GENERAL*

In Washington, after General Ridgway's battlefield successes, the Truman administration felt a profound sense of relief. They now felt that the condition on the ground had stabilized, and that the United Nations forces had even achieved some battlefield victories. They also would no longer have to be concerned about a Dunkirk-style defeat at the hands of the Chinese Communist Army. However, the improved conditions on the ground did not improve the growing tension between General Douglas MacArthur and his circle of advisors, and President Truman and his Joint Chiefs of Staff. It seemed to Truman that MacArthur was becoming even more difficult to deal with. He was openly critical of the Truman administration's war strategy, and condescending and critical about General Ridgway's successes. MacArthur also became more overtly political in his public statements, and in his messages to politicians, many of whom were in the China Lobby, and whom he knew supported his aggressive views on China and the Korean War. He was acting as if he were not only the commander-in-chief of Korean War strategy, but he saw himself as the expert military consultant to the Republican leadership in Congress, as well. General MacArthur, in his statements to the press and to his Republican friends in Congress, stated that the United States, because of the Truman administration's strategy, had lost their will to win in Korea. He openly advocated an all out war with China, and requested additional forces, and even the permission to use atomic weapons, if he thought it was necessary. All of these bellicose statements by MacArthur, to the press and to his political allies, did nothing to improve his relationship with President Truman and the Joint Chiefs of Staff. General MacArthur's reputation was already greatly damaged by the first large Chinese offensive and the resulting retreat of the 8th Army back to the 38th parallel. The Joint Chiefs of Staff and MacArthur's peers in Washington were now paying much less attention to his war strategy recommendations, especially since General Ridgway had been successful in several battles, and had now at least stalemated the Chinese army, in ways that MacArthur had said could not be done.

Back in the United States, the politics of the Korean War seemed to benefit no one. It was a very unpopular war, with many casualties, and with no end in sight. Even with General Ridgway's stalemate of the Chinese Army, the Truman Administration was still embattled with a war that by now was rated very low in public opinion. The longer the war went on, the worse the political consequences would be, not to mention the loss of life of the soldiers fighting the war.

General MacArthur, seemingly oblivious to any reasoning or strategy but his own, showed no interest or concern about the threat that the Russians might pose if his forces again pushed north to the Yalu River, and beyond toward Manchuria. However, with the Cold War at its peak, President Truman was concerned that Russia would use any escalation on the part of U.S. forces, especially when it threatened Manchuria, as an excuse or reason to intervene in the war.

The Truman Administration, disregarding MacArthur, made it clear that the United States was ready to talk, and that they would participate in the initiation of peace talks. They felt that they had neutralized the Chinese advance, won some important battles, and now could enter peace talks from a position of strength. However, to MacArthur, this kind of stalemate was nothing short of a humiliating defeat and he pressed ahead by contacting his Republican allies in Congress. One of these allies was the leader in the House of Representatives, Joe Martin, a passionate backer of Chiang and Formosa, and a member of the China Lobby. The more political the confrontation between MacArthur and Truman became, the faster the situation went from bad to worse. In early April 1951, the Korean War now less than a year old, President Truman met with his senior advisors, and told them directly that General MacArthur had to go.

## THE KOREAN PIPELINE

And so it was that in April 1951, President Truman addressed the nation and told the American people that General MacArthur was being called back from Tokyo and being relieved of his command. He also said that MacArthur was being replaced by General Matthew Ridgway. The reason that President Truman gave for his decision to relieve MacArthur was that he and the General had irreconcilable differences over policy.

PART V
JULY 1951-JULY 1953
ARMISTICE TALKS BEGIN, 1951
ETA JIMA SCHOOL COMMAND
THE CENTRAL CORRIDOR, 1951-1953
THE IRON TRIANGLE
HEARTBREAK RIDGE, 1951
OUTPOST HARRY, 1953
PORK CHOP HILL, 1953
OPERATION LITTLE SWITCH, 1953
ARMISTICE SIGNED, JULY 1953

## *THE ARMISTICE TALKS: KAESONG, 1951*

The armistice talks began at Kaesong in July 1951. Kaesong is a city located in the central part of Korea, and was a former capital of Korea before the country was divided. In 1951, Kaesong came under North Korean control, and its selection as the site for initial peace talks was agreed to by both sides. The talks got started with both sides agreeing on an agenda for the separation of combatants, the constitution of an armistice commission, and a plan for the repatriation of prisoners under the supervision of the International Red Cross. Once the peace talks began, however, the times when both sides were in agreement were few and far between.

The issue of where the cease fire line should be was the first contentious issue to be settled. The Chinese and North Korean Communists wanted the cease fire demarcation line set at the 38$^{th}$ parallel which, as they maintained correctly, was the line from which the war had started. The United Nations delegation responded that since the United States forces had air and sea supremacy that there should be a geographic concession made by the Communists. To emphasize the U.S. air superiority, General Ridgway ordered air attacks on Pyongyang on July 30 and August 10. These attacks, as reported by American and Chinese military, were indiscriminate and caused heavy civilian losses, despite the fact that the United Nations forces had dropped thousands of leaflets warning the civilian population of the impending air strikes. The armistice talks were not getting off to a good start.

The two sides continued to argue over the cease fire line and there were frequent adjournments. There were also military strikes by both sides resulting in the death of soldiers and civilians. General Matthew

Ridgway, known to be a dedicated military hawk, is reported to have decided that to teach the Communists a lesson, further military action was required to bring the enemy "to their senses." General Ridgway was always thinking up new attack plans, even after the cease fire talks began. General officers, such as MacArthur and Ridgway, after all, are taught to make strategic battle plans; it was part of their formal education. Yet what were Ridgway's motives, once peace talks were started, in becoming more aggressive? Was he after more Korean real estate so that the United Nations position at the peace talks would be stronger? Was he attacking the enemy to stage yet another battle campaign to contest a few hundred yards of non-strategic Korean hillside terrain, thereby putting more of his troops at risk; was he out to get another campaign ribbon and battle star to pin on his dress uniform and move up in the chain of command? Was he fully aware and sympathetic to the morale and safety of the troops he ordered into battle while peace talks were underway?

The war dragged on grimly as the armistice talks continued. The only rationale for the continued fighting was to show the enemy that, although a stalemate had been reached and neither side was winning, that the opposing armies would show the other side that they could maintain their positions forever. By the middle of 1952, the Korean War began to resemble the worst of World War I: days of constant artillery fire; trench warfare that included hand-to-hand bayonet fighting; enlisted men with low morale; and all reason for fighting and dying was lost. On top of that, the American officers were always back at Danger Rear reading their maps and coming up with new aggressive battle plans,—plans that they would present to the non-commissioned officers on the front line when they made their infrequent visits to forward positions.

Both sides had developed extensive defensive lines. The Americans had air and artillery supremacy that allowed them to bomb and strafe the enemy indiscriminately, and to drop endless units of napalm. The Chinese, on the other hand, to defend themselves, had adjusted their style of fighting. They built an exceptional system of tunnels that went from their positions of relative safety, forward to the front line of an attack point. These tunnels and new strategy allowed the Chinese infantry to achieve a certain amount of immunity or safety from U.S. airpower.

As the war ground on, there were two struggles that were attempting to be resolved: first, the peace talks at Kaesong which were slow and difficult; and second, the battleground itself, with men dying and being wounded every day. The only objective seemed to be for neither side to "lose face."

# *ETA JIMA SCHOOL COMMAND*

Eta Jima is an island located just off the western coast of Honshu, one of the main Japanese islands. Eta Jima was the former site of the Japanese Naval Academy, that graduated all of Japan's admirals and academy trained officers. In 1946, after World War II, the United States Army took over the island of Eta Jima and the Japanese Naval Academy, and then in 1950 at the start of the Korean War the Army used the academy as a training school for medics and radio/Morse code signalmen.

Eta Jima is a beautiful, small island and the accommodations for military personnel were very comfortable. When Michael Parker arrived at Eta Jima he was impressed by the academic atmosphere and by the competence of the instructors at the school. Parker was assigned to the radio/Morse code school, which was the most difficult course and would last for three months. The course was extensive and required that the students sit in classrooms for eight hours a day, and six of those hours per day were spent listening to Morse code. The instructors often said that if you weren't crazy before you started listening to Morse code all day—with all those dots and dashes coming at you through your ear phones, you would be crazy when you were finished.

Regardless of the rigorous course, Parker knew he was very fortunate to have been selected for this training course. He had been on his way to the Korean front line as an infantry rifleman, so being at Eta Jima was a three month reprieve. It also meant that when he did get assigned to Korea, he would go as a radioman and not as a rifleman. What he soon came to realize, however, was that the life expectancy of a radio operator was not a long one, certainly no longer than that of a rifleman. During the first year of the war the Chinese infantry snipers targeted radio operators and BAR soldiers before anyone else. The American radio operators made a relatively easy target with their radio trucks and high antennae. Nevertheless, Michael Parker felt lucky to be at Eta Jima, and would rather go to Korea as a radio operator than as a rifleman, and he planned to learn all he could about radio technology and procedure.

The following three months at Eta Jima was almost like being back in college for Michael Parker. He studied hard and then took leave on weekends to visit Japanese cities, it was like being a tourist in Japan; the Korean War was hardly on anyone's mind. The weekend trips to Osaka, Hiroshima, Nagasaki, and Tokyo were very interesting and informative, and the Japanese were very friendly. Many of the students at Eta Jima had Japanese girl friends off base, and many of them maintained apartments for them while they were there. The army facilities at Eta Jima also included sports activities such as basketball, softball, and tennis.

Parker made the most of his studies and completed the course in February 1951. He graduated as a high speed radio operator, able to copy code at over 25 words per minute. Today, Morse code is no longer used in radio communication in the armed services; it has been replaced by computers and other high speed communication technology. Nevertheless, back in the 1950s, Morse code was the latest technology and was used extensively in Korea. The radio school at Eta Jima was set up to train radio operators to be sent to combat units in Korea.

After graduating from the school at Eta Jima. Michael Parker was immediately put back in the Korean Pipeline, with all the military protocol and urgency. The relaxed days on Eta Jima were a distant memory, and were replaced by the "hurry up and wait" routine of the army enlisted man. On the train ride from Eta Jima to the port city of Sasebo, Japan, their last stop before arriving in Korea, the men were crowded into makeshift railroad cars, and the meals were routine, at best; some GIs opted for C rations rather than standing in line and eating warmed over hash or Spam out of army mess gear. After arriving at Sasebo, Japan, the men were loaded like cattle onto flat bottom LCIs, or LCTs for the trip across the Korea Strait to Pusan. After several hours on the water, the men got their first sight of Korea from the landing craft, and it was ominous and threatening. The foggy, rough mountainous coastline of South Korea was, at that time, not a friendly sight. Every GI had heard the rumors about Korea, all of them bad, and their first sight of the mainland only reinforced what they had heard. Everyone knew that they were all headed north out of Pusan to the 38$^{th}$ parallel and beyond for their combat assignments.

Once in Pusan, Michael Parker, along with all the other GIs, were loaded onto another crowded troop train, as had Hansen and Foley, and were taken to the front line. Parker was assigned to the 24$^{th}$ Division Artillery, and because he was a high speed operator, he was sent to Headquarters Company; it was late February 1951. There were several firing battalions in the 24$^{th}$ Division and it was Parker's responsibility to send the coded firing messages out to radio operators in the firing battalions, messages to direct fire for the big 115 and 155 howitzers. The rules governing code transmission stated that in a radio network of several operators, the lead operator can transmit code no faster than the slowest operator in the net. That meant that code was usually transmitted at between five and ten words per minute. During the first year of the war there were, unfortunately, times when U.S. forces suffered casualties due to our own artillery firing short rounds, often called friendly fire. During World War II, when the artillery fired short rounds and caused infantry casualties, it was Standard Operating Procedure (SOP) for the responsible firing battery to be summarily relieved, no matter the circumstances. However, in Korea, during the first year of the war, each case of artillery short rounds was handled on its own merits. In most cases, there are extenuating circumstances that are not the fault of the artillery commander, that resulted in friendly fire casualties. One example would be inaccurate reports of troop location due to a constant changing of position. Another probable cause of short rounds was the inaccurate copying of the coded messages by the radio operator. Communication among artillery units was also hampered by mountainous terrain and the constant jamming of U.S. radio communication by Chinese radiomen. Radio communication, voice and Morse code, although sometimes unreliable, was used in Korea with considerable success.

## *THE IRON TRIANGLE*

When Michael Parker joined the 24th Division in February 1951, the United Nations front line, known as the "No Name Line," extended across the Korean peninsula from Seoul to the east coast at a location a few miles north of the 38th parallel. At that time, the U.S. and U.N. forces were using massive air and artillery power to crush Chinese resistance. The 8th Army pushed forward toward an area in the Central Corridor of Korea known as the Iron Triangle. The Iron Triangle was an area of relatively flat land that was surrounded by jagged mountains that protected the enemy's main supply depots. The perimeter locations of the Iron Triangle were formed by the villages of Chorwan, Kumhwa and Kumsong. The name for the Iron Triangle was given to this terrain by American journalists, and the triangle contained a vital network of highways which allowed supplies and reinforcements to support major Communist offensives. The Americans knew that as long as the Iron Triangle remained under Chinese control, every city and strategic area south of the triangle would be at risk. This strategic area, then, was the 8th Army's main objective in February 1951 as they moved toward the base of the Iron Triangle, and then were ordered to dig in and hold their ground. It was into this situation on the ground that Michael Parker reported in February 1951. He was assigned a radio vehicle equipped with voice and carrier wave transmission capabilities. He would be responsible for transmitting the coded firing messages to the big gun battalions, where these messages were decoded and put into action.

In April 1951, General Van Fleet replaced General Ridgway as commander of the 8th Army, and he remained in command until just before the armistice was signed in 1953. Shortly after General Van Fleet took command, U.S. intelligence reported that the Chinese were consolidating their forces and setting up along the Imjin River, in sight of the northern suburbs of Seoul. They had concealed themselves skillfully by day and always moved at night, as they prepared themselves for their next battle. The Americans, in the meantime, and now under the command of General Van Fleet, had regained much of their confidence and pride, knowing that they were backed up by powerful air and artillery support.

It was under these battlefield conditions that the $8^{th}$ Army was ordered to advance on the Iron Triangle. General Van Fleet ordered massive firepower from planes and artillery to crush resistance and spare the number of casualties of his troops. As the Allied advance began to gain momentum, the Chinese counterattacked, and U.S. forces were ordered to hold their ground. Intelligence reports zeroed in on the coordinates where the enemy was expected to be gathering, and Michael Parker was given coded messages to send to the firing battalions.

The situation on the ground remained static for the next several weeks, and then on the evening of May 15, several Chinese and North Korean infantry divisions attacked along the central front, in an area held mainly by Republic of Korea forces. It was the middle of the rainy season in Korea, and the pouring rain reduced the dirt roads to muddy quagmires making it impossible for supply vehicles to reach the troops, or for the artillery to maintain a stable position. After 24 hours of air bombardment and artillery firepower, however, the enemy offensive slowed down and the Chinese were pushed back by Republic of Korea and United Nations forces, and the 8th Army was then ordered to advance on the Iron Triangle.

On May 19, General Van Fleet ordered a full scale offensive against the Chinese forces, and the Americans advanced to the base of the triangle, after their airpower and artillery had rendered severe losses to the enemy. Over 17,000 Chinese are reported to have been killed in action and an equal number were captured.

It was during the May advance on the Iron Triangle that Michael Parker's radio vehicle was hit by mortar fire. The radio equipment was destroyed and Parker was badly injured. He was treated for his injuries at the first aid station in Danger Rear, and then air evacuated by helicopter back to Ascom City, a town near Seoul taken over by the U.S. Army and set up as the headquarters for the 8$^{th}$ Army.

# *ASCOM CITY*

In 1945, after the Japanese surrendered to end World War II, the United States Army took over a former Japanese supply depot and arsenal located at a small town west of Seoul, about halfway to the port of Inchon. This supply depot was built by the Japanese in the mid 1930s to support their troops in Manchuria. After the Americans took over this supply depot they enlarged it considerably, and it became the largest army distribution center in Korea. After 1945, this Army post became a large staging area for United States units stationed along the demilitarized zone, and in 1946 this base acquired the acronym ASCOM (Army Support Command), and then became known to the troops as Ascom City. In July 1950, when the North Koreans invaded South Korea and overran the area along the 38$^{th}$ parallel, they captured Ascom City. From 1950 until 1951, Ascom City changed hands between the North Korean/Chinese forces and the Americans several times as the fighting swept up and down the Korean peninsula. Finally, in the Spring of 1951, the United Nations forces took control of Ascom City permanently, and it became a huge Army base providing supplies and ammunition to United Nations forces. Ascom City also established schools to train army medics and radio technicians for duty in Korea. It was at this time that Michael Parker was assigned to the radio school at Ascom City.

When the Korean War ended, the United States Army Support Command and the Marine Support Command were the major presence at Ascom City. There were no other large supply depots in the Central Corridor of Korea during that time, and Ascom City developed into an important logistical complex, and a supply depot that stockpiled large amounts of supplies and equipment for United Nations forces. In 1972, the phase down of the operation at Ascom City was started, and in 1973 this storage and supply facility ended its operation. Then in June 1973, the United States Army turned the entire Ascom City complex over to the South Korean Ministry of Defense.

## THE CENTRAL CORRIDOR

As the May 1951 offensive on the Iron Triangle continued, the 8th Army was ordered to dig in and prepare a strong defensive perimeter. The soldiers laid thousands of land mines and erected vast fields of barbed wire, and the army engineers built deep trenches and bunkers. It became clear that the new strategy was not to again advance northward and face strong Chinese resistance, or risk possible Soviet intervention; the new strategy was to maintain a static frontline, with only limited advances that would take key ground that would eventually become the demilitarized zone according to the 1953 armistice.

As the static nature of the front line in Korea continued, both sides took time to rebuild their forces. In Washington, President Truman and his advisors refused to authorize any military advance beyond the "Kansas Line," a line stretching from the mouth of the Imjin River eastward across the peninsula, and both sides agreed to halt all major offensive operations. Before this embargo on major offensive operations was established, the 8th Army had succeeded in securing a number of key hill positions in the Iron Triangle, including formerly Communist positions such as the Punchbowl. It was in these well established positions that the 8th Army would dig in and remain for the rest of the war. It was also from these positions that many battles, not deemed to be major offensive operations by the officers who ordered them, would be fought while the peace talks were underway at Panmunjon.

By the end of February 1951, the Chinese and American armies were confronting each other in the Central Corridor of Korea in the area of the Iron Triangle. General Matthew Ridgway had taken over the 8th Army from General Walker in December 1950, and at that time the United

Nations front line was located along the 38th parallel. By January 24, 1951 the front line was located about 50 miles south at about the level of the city of Wonju along the Han River. From February 1951 until the armistice was signed in 1953, the Chinese and American armies fought one another with no obvious objectives, other than to have a stronger position at the armistice talks. Most, if not all, of these battles were initiated by American generals and high level officers; and some of these American commanders even went so far as to state that they were planning these attacks to improve the morale of their fighting men. Did these officers ask their troops if sending them into combat would improve their morale? It would have been more truthful if these officers had stated instead, that they were ordering their troops into combat to add more battle stars to their own personal service record, at the expense of the lives of their front line soldiers. Under General Matthew Ridgway, who ordered many of these battles, the United Nations forces only managed to maintain stalemates with the Chinese forces at Chipyongni and Wonju, and the Americans suffered many casualties. General Ridgway's reputation as a grenade carrying, hard-ass officer, did nothing to gain the respect of the troops he ordered into battle. They thought of him as a "showboat," with slung grenades along his belt and over his shoulder, standing around at the CP in the safety of Danger Rear, trying to look tough as he sent his troops into battle.

    GENERAL RIDGWAY SAYS "HAVE NO FEAR"
    BUT RIDGWAY'S BACK AT DANGER REAR
    WE'RE MOVING ON, WE'RE MOVING ON
    MATT'S GOT NO FEAR, HE'S AT DANGER REAR
    WE'RE MOVING ON

# *PANIC AT THE PUNCHBOWL*

General Van Fleet, following the aggressive example of General Ridgway, was always planning new offensive operations, ostensibly, Van Fleet claimed, to give the American troops more confidence and raise their morale, and also to get the stalled peace talks moving again. Another commander, this one General Hoyt Vandenberg, of the United States Air Force, reportedly never shy about ordering indiscriminate bombing raids, conducted many raids over North Korea while peace talks were in progress, air raids that reportedly only served to strengthen the will of the North Koreans and the Chinese to battle on at all costs.

General Van Fleet had his eye on certain mountain ranges in the Central Corridor, an area known as the Punchbowl, that he deemed to be of strategic value. The North Koreans were deeply dug in along these mountain ranges and they had an excellent vantage point from which to view the American position. General Van Fleet, regardless of intelligence showing a strong, well dug-in defensive perimeter by the enemy, ordered his 8th Army troops to attack this high ground position in the Punchbowl. After several unsuccessful and bloody advances and subsequent retreats, the battle reached a stalemate. It is reported that, again, General Van Fleet was insisting on this campaign strategy so that his troops would acquire more self confidence and to jump start the peace talks. What actually happened was that the area of the Punchbowl became known as Bloody Ridge by the soldiers who fought there, and the 8th Army sustained great losses. The troops under Van Fleet's command were never asked if his battle strategy, and the actual battles that he ordered, did anything to improve their self confidence and morale. If they had been asked, the answer would have been, "Hell, no!" or something more descriptive, such as, "Go fuck yourself, sir!" On the battlefield, the morale of the troops was at rock bottom, and on top of this, the American soldiers who replaced the dead and wounded in the Punchbowl war zone were immediately bewildered and terrified, even before coming under fire. These soldiers had heard from their officers, and actually believed, that the war might be finally winding down; yet here they were being thrown into yet another disastrous battlefield situation by an American general. These replacements arrived at the front knowing no one, and were not able to tell the difference between their Republic of Korea allies and the North Korean enemy. General Van Fleet has the dubious honor, not just at the Punchbowl but during his entire time as commander of the 8th Army, of having high casualty rates for the enlisted men under his command because of his aggressive battle initiatives while peace talks were underway at Panmunjon.

Many aggressive high level officers had high casualty rates for the enlisted men under their command in the Korean War. The fact that these troop loses came with "victories," or at least a stalemate between Chinese and American forces, proved to be enough to move these officers up their command chain. However, it should be noted that these "victories" have to be measured in terms of the questionable objectives of securing small, insignificant hills or ridgelines, or a few hundred yards of non-strategic Korean turf, only to see these hills and ridgelines lost again to the enemy within a few days. Regardless, these "victories" or stalemates, which allowed these officers to achieve their personal goals, were accomplished at the expense of the foot soldiers who fought and died during these battles.

By January 1951, pressure came from Great Britain and the Soviet Union in the United Nations Security Council, to begin talks to explore the possibility of a peaceful ending to the Korean War. However, there was much opposition by the right wing hardliners in the United States Congress, to any talks with the Chinese or Russians. They were opposed to any discussions with the Communists; any talks with the Communists regarding peace in Korea was considered by these hardliners in Washington as tantamount to appeasement or even treason. Those right wing members of the China Lobby were still talking about following

General MacArthur and his plans to charge into Manchuria and onto Russia, if necessary, and always holding out the threat of using atomic weapons if necessary. The China Lobby wanted to wipe out global Communism even if it meant invading China and Russia. Finally, after much discussion pro and con, the Truman administration authorized General Ridgway to make a formal proposal for a meeting between the Americans, on one side, and the Chinese and North Koreans on the other, to discuss cease fire and peace proposals. The meeting was to take place aboard a Danish hospital ship, the Justlandia, located in Wonsan harbor. The Chinese and North Koreans responded by agreeing to hold the meetings, but proposed that the talks be held at the town of Kaesong, instead. After much discussion, both sides agreed on Kaesong as the site for initial discussions, and the date of July 8, 1951 was set for the start of serious negotiations to begin.

## BATTLE OF HEARTBREAK RIDGE, SEPTEMBER-OCTOBER 1951

Many of the battles fought in Korea during this time became well known, and received much attention in the United States; and one of them was the Battle of Heartbreak Ridge. It should be emphasized that this battle and the many to follow, all took place while peace talks were underway; battles that were won and lost while enlisted men died, and after the smoke had cleared on the battlefield there was nothing more to show for their heroism and sacrifice than a few miles of frozen ground and desolate mountain ridges; and these battles and offensive operations were planned and initiated by American generals. Heartbreak Ridge was located in a mountainous area of the Central Corridor in North Korea, and it was the site of a month long fight that took place from September 13 until October 15, 1951. This battle was a continuation of a confrontation at Bloody Ridge in the Iron Triangle, as American and Chinese forces jockeyed for strategic positions in the vicinity of the 38th parallel after the war became stalemated in the summer of 1951.

Within days of the Battle at Bloody Ridge, United States forces attacked the Chinese and North Korean armies along a series of mountain ridges just a few miles north of the previous battles. The fighting is reported to have been savage, with neither side giving in, and with heavy casualties on both sides. The ridgeline under attack by the Americans, and defended by the Chinese and North Koreans, changed hands many times in a series of ferocious attacks and counterattacks. Several American units of company size were completely wiped out in the fighting, and because of these battlefield conditions and loss of men, this mountainous area was named Heartbreak Ridge by the GIs fighting there. The Americans were finally able to employ massive air strikes of bombs and napalm, heavy artillery barrages, and tanks in several attempts to drive the enemy from the ridge.

The fighting along that ridge lasted for 30 days, when finally the Chinese relented and started to withdraw, as the Americans gained the upper hand. The air strikes and artillery had taken their toll on the enemy as they reportedly lost an estimated 25,000 men killed in action. The American losses were estimated at more than 4,000, and may have been under-reported. These heavy losses of American soldiers in battles taking place after peace talks had started, finally began to make a deep impression on the United Nations and United States commands, and they decided that battles such as Heartbreak Ridge were not worth the huge cost in American blood for the extremely small amount of Korean terrain captured. Heartbreak Ridge, however, would not be the last offensive conducted by American forces but it was their last *major* offensive. Sporadic battles along the line of contact between American and Communist forces would continue to be fought right up until the final armistice was signed in July 1953.

## *THE BATTLE OF HILL EERIE, 1952*

Hill Eerie was a military outpost about ten miles west of Chorwan, at the base of the Iron Triangle. During the first year of the war Hill Eerie changed hands many times as Chinese/North Korean forces and the American Army fought up and down the Korean peninsula. In March 1952, Hill Eerie was under the responsibility of the United States Army 45th Infantry Division, and on March 21, they set out to take over Hill Eerie. The American unit consisted of a platoon of 26 men that included two rifle squads, a light machine gun squad, and a 60mm mortar squad. Two patrol squads were deployed to set up an ambush site around the hill. That night these two patrol squads made contact with the Chinese infantry, and both sides fought a machine gun duel; the Americans were supported by heavy mortar fire. The battle continued throughout the night, and with the support of air strikes and artillery barrages the Americans prevailed, advanced on Hill Eerie and retook the position. The casualties were heavy on both sides with the Americans losing eight men killed in action and four wounded; the enemy lost 31 killed in action and several were wounded.

In May and June 1952, Hill Eerie was the site of more battles during which the American forces were able to hold their ground and turn back the Chinese attacks. The success of these battles was aided by the American F-86 Sabre jets that dropped ordnance and napalm on the enemy, and by the heavy artillery barrage that stopped their advance. These battles were the final confrontations between the Communist and American forces at Hill Eerie during the rest of the

Korean War. Again, these battles were fought with no objective in mind, other than a few hundred yards of desolate Korean terrain, as American enlisted men, following orders, were wounded and killed in action.

# *OUTPOST HARRY, 1953*

Outpost Harry was also located along the base of the Iron Triangle In Korea, and was the scene of many battles in the Central Corridor during the war. This outpost got its name from a United Nations/Greek Expeditionary Force that called this terrain Outpost Haros, the Greek name for Death. This Greek Expeditionary Force suffered heavy losses in the fighting at Outpost Harry.

The Chinese and Americans faced each other once again at Outpost Harry in June 1953, and both sides were supported by heavy mortar and artillery fire. The enemy anticipated an easy victory, and they sent waves of infantrymen against the United Nations forces. After eight days of intense fighting, including hand-to-hand combat, the Chinese could not endure more losses in supplies and manpower, having suffered more than 4,200 killed in action and 1,000 wounded. During this period of fighting most of the battles were conducted at night, while the daylight hours were usually spent taking care of the dead and wounded, reinforcing their company strength, sending up supplies, and repairing their defensive perimeters. Finally on the night of June 17, the fighting resumed and both sides attempted to move through artillery and mortar fire to advance on Outpost Harry from their respective positions. The enemy was turned back and forced to withdraw, although they stayed in the area. The fighting continued and again led to hand-to-hand combat with the enemy making numerous attempts to overrun Outpost Harry. The Americans finally prevailed and turned back the Chinese, although these victories had a hollow ring to them, considering the loss of American lives, and the fact that a final Armistice signing was only days away.

# THE BATTLE OF PORK CHOP HILL

In 1953, with peace talks underway in Panmunjon and making no obvious progress, the war ground on grimly; the only purpose was to show the other side that each army could stay there forever. The war had begun to resemble the worst of World War I: with trench warfare; hand-to-hand combat with fixed bayonets; constant artillery and mortar barrages; days and nights of existing under constant tension; combat fatigue spreading among the troops; and there was almost no meaning whatsoever to the fighting and dying.

By this time of the Korean War, the Chinese had developed virtually unassailable defensive lines, and because of the American air and artillery supremacy, they developed an extensive network of tunnels that went from Chinese positions in their rear areas to the very point of an attack location. The Chinese also had their artillery hidden away, virtually invisible from the air and therefore not vulnerable to attack by United States planes. The artillery were usually located in caves on the far side of the mountains for the purpose of shielding them from attack, and they were able to wheel their artillery pieces out of the caves, fire 20 or 30 rounds on American positions, and then wheel their big guns back into the cave.

As the war continued under these circumstances, the peace talks were moving at a slow and difficult pace, while soldiers on both sides were being killed in action. The only objective to the fighting seemed to be that neither side was going to lose "military face." It was under these conditions that the Battle of Pork Hill was fought in the Spring of 1953.

Pork Chop Hill was the nickname for another American outpost in the Iron Triangle where many battles took place, and the intensity of these battles was affected by the way that the peace talks were progressing; the closer the opposing sides were to reaching an agreement at Panmunjon, the more the value of Pork Chop Hill and other outposts seemed to go up as a strategic goal to maintain and defend, and the bloodier the fighting became.

Pork Chop Hill is most accurately described as a series of battles, battles that had been going on for more than a year, with the hill outpost changing hands several times. These battles became a symbol of the emptiness and cruel stupidity of the last and final stages of the Korean War. So much had been invested in this war for so little gain, and Pork Chop Hill was just another example of a bloody and bitter battle that should not have been fought. It involved a small number of infantry units, at the outer edges of the United Nations lines, who were struggling to hold a distant, non-strategic outpost; non-strategic, that is, except to General Matthew Ridgway and his advisors in Tokyo, who did not want to lose face to their adversary, and ordered these battles be fought at the expense of their troops.

In March 1953, the Chinese were defending Pork Chop Hill and were driven off, but during their withdrawal the enemy captured a neighboring outpost called Old Baldy, which made Pork Chop Hill that much more vulnerable. The situation on the ground remained stalemated until mid-April when the Chinese counterattacked, this time with more than 2,300 infantrymen. What followed was a ferocious ground battle as the Americans were supported by an overwhelming artillery barrage. According to military historian S.L.A. Marshall in his book about Pork Chop Hill, the artillery battle lasted two days and expended more artillery rounds and final output of weapons, than any battle ever fought during World War II. The American troops managed to hold Pork Chop Hill during the April attack, and the situation again remained at a stalemate until July 1953 when the fighting resumed once again. The ensuing battle was ferocious and lasted for five days, fighting again to a virtual stalemate, as hundreds more men were killed in action. Finally, on the morning of July 11, after days of monitoring the fighting from the safety of his position well behind the front line, General Maxwell Taylor ordered that the Americans could withdraw from the battle; that Pork

Chop Hill was not worth the investment of any more American lives, and that the battle of Pork Chop Hill was over. The surviving Americans slowly withdrew from the ridgeline, and returned to the safety of their units. It will be up to civilian historians, not military historians, to determine whether General Taylor exercised good judgment in allowing Americans GIs to continue fighting and dying when the only objective was a few hundred feet of a desolate ridgeline in Korea.

## *OPERATION LITTLE SWITCH*

Before a peace agreement could be reached in Korea, the political process in the United States had to come to terms with the idea of the war ending in a stalemate. When General Eisenhower took office in 1953, he appeared to be the perfect centrist Republican president that could bring home a peace settlement that a Democratic president could not. President Eisenhower was thoughtful, careful, and experienced, and although he was an aggressive military strategist, he was the least jingoistic of military men at that time. He was what the United States needed during those days, a tempering figure at a dangerous time, and he wanted to get out of Korea. Then in March 1953, Joseph Stalin died, opening the way for a final peace solution in Korea. Both the Americans and the Chinese could now reach a settlement that had previously alluded them. President Eisenhower was able to support a peace settlement that involved a stalemate that the Truman administration could not; and the Chinese, now without Joseph Stalin looking over their shoulder, were able to proceed as well.

Then on April 1953, an exchange of prisoners was set up known as Operation Little Switch. This set the stage for further substantial talks and progress. However, there remained many problems, and one of the major impediments was Syngman Rhee himself. Rhee was against a stalemate end to the war; he wanted the country united under his rule regardless of the loss of life; and so he attempted to undermine the peace talks. But no matter what Syngman Rhee tried to do, he was not able to stop the peace process that was gathering momentum, and was backed by President Eisenhower. The major powers in the Korean War wanted out; the fact that the war was finally ending was now inevitable.

## ARMISTICE TALKS: PANMUNJON, 1951-1953

By August 1951, the cease fire talks had been moved to Panmunjon, a city located in the central part of Korea, about at the level of the 38th parallel. At that time the United Nations defensive line ran from the mouth of the Imjin River on a westward track across the peninsula. The months dragged on, and by the summer of 1952 no real progress had been made. Both sides were making allegations against the other in an effort to gain advantage in the negotiations. When it became apparent that the truce talks were going to last a long time, a base camp was set up at Munsan, a town south of Panmunjon. This camp became the headquarters for the world press corps from where both sides tried to influence world opinion.

One of the major deterrents to progress at the peace talks was the issue of prisoner repatriation. Both sides were accusing the other of torturing prisoners and not abiding by the Rules of the Geneva Convention. The Geneva Convention of 1949 laid down instructions of conduct for captors and prisoners, and emphasized that prison camps should be periodically inspected by a neutral organization. However, in 1950 the United States, the North Korean Peoples Republic, and China had not signed the Geneva Convention. The North Koreans regarded prisoners as a source of forced labor and a possible source of intelligence information. The prisoners were also used for political indoctrination. The Chinese policy offered the prisoners the option of receiving political education which, if not accepted, could result in beatings, starvation, lack of medical care, and solitary confinement.

The armistice agreement had a provision for the repatriation of prisoners. Those prisoners who refused to return to their country were allowed to live under a neutral supervising commission for three months. At the end of this three month period, those prisoners who still refused repatriation would be released. There are no definite numbers for captured North Korean and Chinese prisoners who refused repatriation. Among the United Nations prisoners of war who refused repatriation were 22 American and British soldiers, all but two of whom chose to defect to the People's Republic of China.

The armistice also established a four kilometer wide demilitarized zone (DMZ) along the 38th parallel, and although most troops and all heavy equipment were to be removed from the DMZ, the area just outside the demilitarized zone has been heavily armed by both sides since the end of the fighting.

The peace talks at Panmunjon took place in several tents that were set up on the north side of the road that connects Kaesong and Seoul. The armistice agreement was contained in two volumes of documents, and was signed by the Senior Delegates of the opposing sides in a building that was constructed just for the signing ceremony. After the cease fire agreement was signed, construction was started on a new negotiating site that was approximately one kilometer from the previous site. This new location was called the Joint Security Area (JSA), and from that time on all meetings between the Communists and the United Nations Command took place in this JSA building. After the war, when all civilians were removed from the DMZ, the village of Panmunjon, now without inhabitants, fell into disrepair and there is no evidence of it today. However, the building constructed for the signing of the armistice has since been renamed by North Korea as the Peace Museum, and it remains as a tourist attraction to this day.

The final agreement was signed by the United Nations, the United States, China and North Korea. However, South Korea, uncompromising in its demand for a unified nation, refused to sign the armistice agreement. South Korea's refusal to sign the armistice did nothing to stop the cease fire from going into effect; even though the fighting had ended, however, North Korea and South Korea were technically still at war.

Panmunjon was the center of one of the world's most tense military and political fault lines, and therefore has been the location of several high profile incidents. During August 1976, North Korean guards attacked a United Nations security team. There had been disputes between opposing check points over visability across the DMZ, and two American officers were killed during this incident. Then on August 21, 1976, three days later, the Americans conducted a military operation called Operation Paul Bunyon, a massive show of force to reassert the United Nations right to conduct military operations on their side of the DMZ. During this operation, several North Korean tunnels were discovered; tunnels that were used for troop infiltration purposes and for their own protection from American bombing, strafing and napalm attacks.

On December 23, 1968, the captured crew of the U.S.S. Pueblo were returned to the United States through Panmunjon, and across the DMZ. They had been held in captivity for eleven months.

A number of defections have taken place over the years. The most recent was that of a Senior Captain of the North Korean Army in February 1998.

# PART VI
# CONTROVERSIAL AND COMPELLING ISSUES
# THAT AFFECTED THE KOREAN WAR

## CONGRESS AND THE KOREAN WAR

The initial reaction of the United States Congress to President Truman's decision to commit American troops to fight and die in Korea was to unite behind the President. However, Truman did not ask for a formal declaration of war, which turned out to be a huge political mistake. President Truman even tried to downplay the significance of sending young Americans to war, by actually referring to the war at a press conference as a "police action." Had Truman obtained a formal declaration of war, it probably would not have prevented much of the criticism about his handling of the war, but it would have made Congress share the responsibility for the developing quagmire in Korea, for the Americans being killed in action, and for the long stalemate which followed.

On June 29, 1950, right after the war started, Congress passed a law that expanded the amount of military and monetary assistance that the United States would provide to the South Korean army, and then in September 1950, Congress passed the Defense Production Act which implemented most of Truman's requests for economic mobilization. Congress also passed Defense Appropriation Acts in 1951 and 1952, which essentially gave to President Truman anything he asked for. However, as the war ground on, and with American casualties mounting every day, President Truman and his allies in the Congress, ran into harsh political criticism from the Republicans, who had little sympathy for "Truman's War." And then, when the Chinese entered the war, everything went from bad to worse, both in Korea and in the United States where support for the war was going up in smoke. There was very little political unity for the President or for the Korean War in 1950 and 1951.

During that time, both Houses of Congress were debating the Korean War, and it became a widely held belief that the Soviet Union was behind what was happening in Korea. The China Lobby became prominent, and these right wing hardliners, who saw Communist conspiracies everywhere, were blaming the President, not only for everything that was happening in Korea but also for losing Chiang Kai-shek's China to the Communist government on the Chinese mainland. Senator Joseph McCarthy, the self-proclaimed anti-communist crusader in the Senate, and his colleague Roy Cohn were loudly claiming that China was lost to the Communists because disloyal Americans had prevented Chiang Kai-shek from receiving the aid he needed to defeat Red China, and now Chiang was isolated on Taiwan. The China Lobby and Senator Joseph McCarthy also claimed that American soldiers were dying in Korea because they had been betrayed by disloyal liberal politicians who had turned China over to the Communists. The China Lobby was pushing the President to be more aggressive against the Chinese in Korea, and to use whatever military means were at our disposal, including atomic weapons, to "wipe out global Communism in Asia, before it spreads to the United States." They advocated going full speed ahead, through China and even into Moscow, to end what they saw as a threat to the American civilization.

In the meantime, the battlefield situation in Korea was going from bad to worse, with General MacArthur making one miscalculation after another—and then he began questioning the authority and strategy of President Truman and his advisors. Not long after that, President Truman fired General MacArthur, and the political support Truman had at that time evaporated. Regardless of all the disastrous decisions and miscalculations that MacArthur had made in Korea, his dismissal was extremely unpopular in the Congress, and led to Congress refusing to approve Truman's request for extending and strengthening his presidential war powers under the Defense Production Act. Many in Congress began to voice their opposition by publicly calling for the president's impeachment. Some members of Congress argued that the President was seeking unconstitutional and dictatorial powers, and that his unilateral intervention into Korea was not authorized. President

Truman and the Democratic Congress were consistently attacked by the Republicans in Congress, and by the time Truman left the White House in 1952, he was one of the most unpopular presidents in American history.

President Dwight Eisenhower, who replaced Truman, was able to negotiate an armistice agreement which stopped the fighting, six months after he took office. Eisenhower, who had made his mark in the military, turned out to be an excellent president for the times, and a formidable military man, while he was in office.

## THE GREAT BUG OUT

During the first year of the Korean War, the United States Army was under-strength, poorly trained, inadequately armed, and under supplied. The young Americans sent to Korea in the early months of the war had no idea of what they were about to encounter on the battlefield. They were being told by their officers that now that the Americans were in the war, the enemy would probably lay down their arms and surrender. These young enlisted men believed what their officers were telling them, so it was a shock for them when the battlefield reality hit them. The North Korean Army was well trained, well equipped, and highly motivated, and when they invaded South Korea, their T-34 tanks and infantry rolled over everything in their way. These young American soldiers were thrown into battle, by the high level officers in Tokyo to slow down the North Korean assault, and to give the United States time to build up their forces. So it was, that under these battlefield conditions—an unprepared, untrained American army faced an advancing well-trained, formidable enemy led by T-34 tanks—that many of these troops broke from their battle lines, and along with a complete lack of officer leadership, they retreated from the enemy and headed south toward Pusan.

The 24th Division was the first American unit into Korea, and the 24th had an almost complete turnover in personnel, all of them killed in action. The terms "The Great Bug Out" or "Bug Out Fever" were used very often during the first year of the war when talking about the American retreat and withdrawal in front of the North Korean onslaught, and then, again, after the Chinese entered the war, and the Americans had to retreat back to the 38th parallel. The American GI knew that many units were breaking ranks and heading for the rear, to break away from the oncoming North Korean and Chinese assault. It was a chaotic scene, an enlisted man's nightmare, a battlefield situation that left everyone on their own. There was also a complete void in officer leadership; the only time a GI saw an officer was when the officer was leading a withdrawal toward the rear; they were never seen on point when advancing on the enemy.

In Washington, D.C., the Joint Chiefs of Staff along with hundreds of other high level non-combat officers, very safely settled in their offices in the Pentagon, were expressing outrage that American troops would run away from a fight. Very few of these officers had ever seen combat in World War II, and if they had they were always safely located behind the front lines, and they certainly hadn't seen combat in Korea,—so for them to express outrage over what young American enlisted men were doing to survive in Korea was, in itself, outrageous. These high-level officers back at the Pentagon were looked upon by the soldiers on the front line in Korea, as nothing more than "pampered sissies," sitting back in Washington, D.C. counting their medals.

Mort Sahl, comedian and political satirist, often poked fun at politicians and high level military officers. It was during the Vietnam War when Mort was making fun of the military, and he probably had General Westmoreland in mind when he said, "All these medals these generals wear, you know, all over their dress uniforms? Very, very impressive!!— Very impressive, if you're twelve years old!" And late night comedians sometimes commented on these military officers. "These generals are in great shape, you know—well, they have to be in great shape, to be able to stand up straight with all those goddamn medals hanging all over their uniforms."

The Pentagon, always attempting to appear forceful and in control, issued a memo in August 1950, just two months after the North Korean invasion, complaining that the American soldiers in Korea "lacked an aggressive spirit," and that they were not "up to World War II fighting standards." This memo was an outrageous lie, and written at a time when 400 to 500 American enlisted men were being killed in action each week in Korea. These same officers tried to blame the Republic of Korea army for the American defeat and withdrawal; these same officers even tried to blame the Doolittle Board, claiming that the Board's decisions led to a weakening of U.S. Army structure and discipline; these same officers were also quick to falsely place the blame for "The Great Bug Out" on segregated infantry units. These blatant rascist attacks by high-level officers were absolutely false. "Bug Out Fever" affected all fighting men the same during the first terrible months on the battlefields of Korea.

After the initial invasion by the North Koreans was stopped at the Pusan Perimeter, and after the success of the Inchon Landing, the United Nation forces, under orders from General MacArthur, headed north across the 38th parallel, and toward the Yalu River and Manchuria. It was then, in November 1950, that the Chinese Dragon entered the war with overwhelming force, and American and United Nations forces were again forced to withdraw, sometimes in disorganized full flight. The facts on the ground were that the Chinese infantrymen appeared to be swarming everywhere, firing their infamous "burp guns"; the United Nations and American forces had disastrous leadership, from MacArthur down to the CP in Danger Rear; and the only choice that the American and Republic of Korea forces had, was to withdraw to the south of Korea. These withdrawals were sometime fairly well executed, and sometimes these withdrawals were completely disorganized. The United Nations retreat to the south in front of the Chinese army became known as "The Great Bug Out," and American GI morale was extremely low, if not non-existent. Months later, in April 1951, General Matthew Ridgway assumed command of the 8th Army after General Walker's death in a jeep accident, and he is given some credit for taking control of the battlefield situation and raising troop morale. However, given the circumstances under which General Walker had to command the 8th Army, he did extremely well, and General Ridgway, under these same conditions would have fared no better than General Walker.

"The Great Bug Out" was a controversial aspect of the Korean War in its early months. The Pentagon came out strongly blaming the troops, the Republic of Korea army, the segregated infantry units, and even the Doolittle Board. This was an excellent example of high level officers attempting to pass the blame to everyone except themselves for their own leadership failures. The entire blame for "The Great Bug Out" should be laid where it belongs, right at the feet of the Truman administration, the Joint Chiefs of Staff, the high-level officers at the Pentagon, and the other high-level officers in General MacArthur's Tokyo office. The decision to send unprepared, untrained, and ill-equipped enlisted men into battle against what these officers knew was a formidable North Korean army, and then the decision to head north after Inchon to the Manchurian border and threaten the Chinese, were both disastrous decisions for which the American enlisted man paid the ultimate price. The blame for "The Great Bug Out" belongs entirely with the military leadership that allowed this to happen, and to this day, no one has been held accountable for the huge number of American casualties that were a direct result of these decisions.

In short, during the first months of the Korean War, months that included demoralizing defeats for American forces and "The Great Bug Out" that followed, the heroes were the enlisted men on the ground, who in the face of overwhelming odds managed to slow down the enemy advance on Pusan. And then, after the entry of the Chinese into the war in November 1950, these enlisted men were again courageous; they were heroes in the face of the Chinese juggernaut that they were completely unprepared for, and had been ordered into battle by their leaders, leaders who were always safely back in Danger Rear or in Tokyo. The real cowards, in the first weeks and months of the war, during the North Korean invasion and the Chinese entry into the war, were the high-level officers at the Pentagon, along with the cadre of incompetent officers in Tokyo—led by General Douglas MacArthur.

WE'RE BUGGING OUT, WE'RE GETTING OUT OF HERE
WE'RE HEADING BACK TO DANGER REAR
WE'RE MOVING ON, WE'RE MOVING ON
WE'RE BUGGING OUT TODAY, GET OUT OF MY WAY
WE'RE MOVING ON.

# THE UNITED STATES AIR FORCE

With the creation of the United States Air Force (USAF) in the late 1940s, as a separate military arm, and with the advent of atomic weapons, many political and military leaders sought to consolidate the power of the Air Force and rely solely on air power, and atomic weapons if necessary, to win wars. And when North Korea invaded South Korea, the generals in the new Air Force Command, saw this as an opportunity to show that air power was the answer to regional and global conflicts. At this time, in the summer of 1950, the United States Air Force was less than three years old, and the Korean War was their first conflict as an independent military service.

During the occupation of Japan after World War II, the branch of the United States Air Force that was responsible for aerial defense was the Far East Air Force (FEAF), commanded by Lt. General George Stratemeyer. And it was one of these FEAF flight squadrons, under the command of Major General Earle Partridge, that was first sent to Korea. The first United States Air Force plane destroyed in the war was a C-54 transport that was hit by enemy fighters at Seoul's Kimpo Airfield. During the course of the war, more than 1,400 USAF planes and 900 enemy aircraft would be lost in battle, and less than ten percent of these losses were due to air-to-air combat. The primary mission of the USAF during the first months of the war was defensive, mostly protecting transport aircraft and ships carrying civilian refugees and the military that were evacuating Korea.

By July 1950, the United States Air Force had achieved air supremacy over North Korea, and that rendered the enemy air force incapable of effective interference in the skies over Korea. However, that air

## THE KOREAN PIPELINE

supremacy did not last long. In November 1950, while General MacArthur was predicting victory as he ordered the 8th Army north toward the Yalu River and Manchuria, suddenly the Chinese entered the battle on the ground and in the air, and drove the United Nations forces back to a location that was south of the 38th parallel. The Chinese Air Force entered the battle as well, with Russian made MiG-15 jet fighters. With the abrupt appearance of this new and very dangerous adversary, the air war entered a new phase.

The MiG-15 jets were far superior to any aircraft in the United States Air Force inventory at that time, and the MiG pilots were also well trained, some of whom were veteran Russian pilots. The USAF soon sent a counter aircraft, the F-86 Sabre jet, into battle against the MiGs; and many of the Sabre jet pilots were veterans of World War II. It wasn't long before the F-86 Sabre jets and MiG-15s were mixing it up in the skies over northwest Korea, in an area that became known as MiG Alley.

While the war on the ground turned into a stalemate by late Spring 1951, MiG Alley remained a hot spot for MiGs versus Sabre jets throughout the war, right up until the armistice was signed. The U.S. Air Force continued to send B-29s on bombing runs over North Korea by day, until the enemy MiG-15s shot down five Superfortress B-29s during one week in October 1950. Since these B-29s were shot down during a day raid, these bombing runs in the future were done only at night. Day after day, however, the Sabre jet F-86s and F-84 Thunderjets swept into MiG Alley to meet the MiG-15s that zoomed up from their bases in Manchuria. Although these Manchurian bases were off limits to U.S. aircraft, some of the American jets occasionally strayed across the border in "hot pursuit" of MiG aircraft. It should be noted that enemy sanctuaries in Manchuria was a hot topic back in Washington, D.C. at that time. Many in Congress and at the Pentagon, and especially the hardliners in the infamous China Lobby, were urging the Truman administration to lift the ban on these sanctuaries and send bombing runs into Manchuria. What these hardliners didn't take into acount (out of arrogance or ignorance), was the fact that the United States had their own sanctuaries in South Korea and Japan, such as Yokahama, Tokyo, and other large cities where American troops were stationed. These cities would have been within range of enemy aircraft, and would have been easy targets for Chinese fighter planes and bombers. Regardless of the controversy back in Washington, D.C., the sanctuaries in Manchuria and those in Japan remained under an attack ban by both sides during the conflict.

Once peace talks had started, rather than slow down the number and ferocity of battles on the ground, these battles continued to be fought, with a few hundred yards of meaningless terrain being won and lost by both sides, while American enlisted men continued to die in battle. The U.S. Air Force, as their aircraft arsenal enlarged, also began to increase their attacks. They continued to bomb bridges, warehouses, railroads, and other targets in North Korea. The bombers also dropped anti-personnel bombs and saturated North Korea with napalm fire-gel cannisters. These operations were given names such as STRANGLE and SATURATE, and their purpose was to paralyze the enemy's transportation system upon which they relied for supplies. Many of these bombing missions were hampered by bad weather, and also by MiG interceptors. It has been reported by military and civilian historians that these air attacks often served to increase the resolve of the North Koreans and Chinese, who went on to build extensive underground defenses. It is also reported that many of these American air attacks and bombing runs were indiscriminate, and that the bombs and saturation napalm attacks often wiped out large civilian refugee populations. The pilots were told by their commanders that very often the enemy used these refugee groups to hide their infantry and infiltrators, and that therefore could be fired upon. Some pilots refused to carry out these directives, while other pilots followed orders, and they have documented in their logs the extent of damage leveled on these groups.

The U.S. Air Force attacks continued unabated while peace talks went on. These raids over North Korea included bombing runs on four hydro-electric generating complexes in areas close to the Yalu River and the Manchurian border in June 1952. Then in June 1953, just weeks short of the signing of the armistice, American planes bombed and shattered three of North Korea's irrigation dams causing extensive flooding that wiped out roads, railroad tracks, thousands of acres of rice fields, and drowned large numbers of refugees. These bombing runs created a massive refugee crises in North Korea, with civilians fleeing their homes and farms, not knowing which way to go for their safety.

The ferocity and magnitude of the air war conducted by the U.S. Air Force is revealed in a statistical summary issued by the military. In June 1950, the Air Force in Korea consisted of 33,000 personnel; by July 1953, the Air Force was increased four times to more than 115,000 officers and airmen. In the summer of 1950, the Air Force consisted of 44 squadrons and more than 650 aircraft; by the summer of 1952, the Air Force grew to 70 squadrons and 1440 aircraft. During the war the Americans flew more than 720,000 sorties and delivered 476,000 tons of ordnance, and it is estimated by the military that these raids accounted for more than 150,000 North Korean and Chinese soldiers killed in action. The civilian casualties are estimated to be well over 100,000, and the number of refugees created by these bombing runs is estimated to be several hundred thousand.

In 1950, at the beginning of the Korean War, the U.S. Air Force saw the war as a means of consolidating its power as a newly designated separate military service. It did not want to be subordinate to the Army again. Air Force leaders attempted to convince Washington D.C. that through air power and the atomic bomb, the United States could maintain complete military superiority over all nations; and that no one would challenge the United States under these circumstances. This has proven to be a false assumption, and military historians have noted that what Air Force leaders failed to consider was that no one in the United States government would ever have the "courage" to use nuclear weapons after World War II; and these historians emphasized again, what history has proven to be correct: that bombing alone will not defeat an enemy; it takes air power along with troops on the ground to achieve victory.

The Korean War was the first time that the army helicopter was used extensively in conflict. Helicopters such as the YR-4 were used in World War II, but their use was rare, and it was the Jeep Willys MB that was the main method for evacuating wounded soldiers from the battlefield. In the Korean War, helicopters such as the H-19 were used extensively to air evacuate injured troops back to army hospitals. During the first year of the war it was not unusual to see helicopters flying overhead carrying open "caskets" with injured soldiers in them, on their way to a medical station.

The helicopter proved to be a valuable military asset during the Korean War. After World War II, improvements were made to helicopters, and they were tested in combat in Korea. The need for close air support helicopters eventually led to the development of the AH-1 Cobra gunship that was used extensively in the Vietnam conflict. Helicopters like those used in the Korean War for troop movement and Medevac missions, were also seen to work well in combat, and these designs were improved upon. The combat experience in Korea for helicopters was very important to the development of the military helicopter gun ships.

The United States Air Force entered the Korean War in July 1950 as a relatively new separate branch of the military, and they continued the air war over Korea for three years, until finally on July 27, 1953, the armistice was signed and the war was over.

# *MIG ALLEY*

MiG Alley was the name that was given by American pilots during the Korean War to the northwestern portion of North Korea, where the Yalu River runs westward and empties into the Yellow Sea. MiG Alley was formed in the shape of a rectangle whose boundaries were noted by Changju on the Yalu River to the northeast, Muichon on the southeast corner, Sinanju on the southwest corner on the Yellow Sea, and Sinuiju on the northwest corner and on the Yalu River. During the Korean War this area was the site of numerous "dogfights" between American F-86 Sabre jets and the Russian built MiG-15 jets, and is considered to be the birthplace of jet fighter combat.

In the first months of the Korean War the Americans maintained complete air supremacy over the North Koreans, who had a small, obsolete air force of propeller driven Soviet aircraft. For several months, the Americans roamed the skies over North Korea virtually at will using F-80 Shooting Stars and F-84 Thunderjet fighters. The United States also sent their B-29 bombers on extensive bombing runs over North Korea, and they were virtually uncontested. However, in October 1950, the Soviet Union agreed to provide air regiments of Russian designed and built MiG-15 jet fighters. These MiG jets were state-of-the-art aircraft, and the Kremlin also agreed to provide training for the Chinese and North Korean pilots. From that time on until the Armistice was signed in July 1953, the air war over North Korea changed considerably.

Soviet MiG air regiments were based on Chinese airfields in Manchuria, where, according to the existing rules of engagement, they could not be attacked by U.S. aircraft. The MiG pilots also operated under tight rules of engagement, and were prohibited from flying over non-communist controlled territory or within 30 to 50 miles of the American front lines. They were also prohibited from sending bombing raids on Japanese cities and American air bases. The mission of the MiG fighters was to defeat or deter the large-scale daylight B-29 bombing raids on North Korea by the Americans, and it is reported that the enemy was largely successful in achieving this objective. After the MiGs entered the war, the Americans sent heavier fighter escorts with the B-29s, but this failed to cut their losses. The MiG pilots learned quickly how to pick off the lumbering, slow moving B-29s, and the B-29 fleet losses mounted throughout the spring and summer of 1951. The successful efforts of the MiG aircraft climaxed during the air battle of October 23, 1951, when it is reported that more than 100 MiG-15 jets attacked a convoy of B-29s and their escorts. This air fight was called "Black Thursday" by the Americans, as the United States lost three B-29s shot down, four crash landed in South Korea, and three more were judged to be beyond repair upon returning to their base.

After "Black Thursday," the daylight raids were discontinued, and the B-29s were only sent out at night, but these night raids also turned out to be deadly. On June 10, 1952, the Americans lost five more B-29s during a night raid, with one Superfortress reported to have exploded in mid-air, and another was forced to crash land at Kimpo Airfield, near Seoul. Although the Americans were outnumbered in the MiG air conflict, the F-86 Sabre pilots did have some advantages. They had a radar ranging gun sight on their six .50 caliber machine guns which ensured that they hit the target. The F-86 pilots were also equipped with G-suits, which prevented pilot blackout in high speed turning maneuvers. The American pilots developed a great deal of respect for their MiG opponents, and nicknamed them "honchos," the Japanese word for "big shot."

The MiG Alley battles produced American fighter aces and MiG-15 pilot aces. The top U.S. ace of the war was Captain Joseph McConnell, who claimed 16 MiGs. Hollywood immortalized him in a film "The Mc Connell Story" starring Alan Ladd and June Allyson. Another American fighter pilot was Major Fred "Boots" Blesse, who shot down nine MiG-15s, and later wrote "No Guts, No Glory," a manual of fighter pilot combat that is still studied today. The enemy had their pilot aces as well, and according to military reports, two Soviet fighter pilots shot down 21 and 19 American aircraft respectively. The casualty statistics over MiG Alley remain controversial, and may never be confirmed. However, the United States claims to have shot down more than 379 MiG-15s, and the Chinese/North Koreans claim to have shot down more than 1,000 United Nations planes. The United States admits to losing less than 200 aircraft in aerial combat over MiG Alley.

MiG Alley achieved fame and notoriety during the Korean War, and the bombing runs and "dog fights" continued even though peace talks were underway. The extent and ferocity of the air war began to abate, however, during the spring of 1953 shortly before the armistice was signed. One of the reasons for this was the death of Joseph Stalin; that's when the new Soviet leadership began signaling the Eisenhower administration in Washington that "a way out" should be found to this seemingly endless war.

# NUCLEAR WEAPONS AND THE KOREAN WAR

On November 30, 1950, President Truman remarked at a press conference that the use of atomic weapons was under active consideration. The President came under a storm of protest for these remarks, and he quickly pointed out that only he could authorize the use of atomic weapons, and that he had not given that authorization. President Truman was seeking to allay the fears that many United States politicians and foreign leaders had regarding the possibility that the use of these weapons would be left to the discretion of General MacArthur, who many believed was not reliable and could not be trusted with decisions of this magnitude. However, on the day of this news conference, orders were sent to top Air Force generals of the Strategic Air Command (SAC) to "augment SAC capacity to include atomic capabilities."

The concern of foreign leaders that the United States was getting ready to use atomic weapons prompted a meeting on December 4, 1950 with British Prime Minister Clement Atlee, French Prime Minister Rene' Pleven and his Foreign Minister Robert Schuman to discuss their concerns over the possible use of atomic weapons. Political leaders in Australia and Canada were insisting that General MacArthur be held to strict controls. India supported a cease fire, and maintained that the Chinese intervention was defensive in nature, a move to protect their borders. Then on December 6, 1950, after the Chinese had entered the war and forced the American and United Nations armies into a retreat from North Korea, there was a meeting in MacArthur's Tokyo office that included the Army Chief of Staff, General Lawton Collins, General MacArthur and other high level staff officers to determine what their options were, and what strategic moves should be taken against the Chinese. The meeting in the Tokyo office developed three potential strategies and outcomes.

The first scenario was that if the Chinese attack continued and the United States forces were still forbidden to mount air attacks in Manchuria; and if no reinforcements were sent to Korea by Chiang Kai-shek; and if there was no substantial increase in United States forces until April 1951; then under these circumstances the atomic bomb would be used in North Korea.

The second scenario assumed that the Chinese attack would continue; air attacks on the Chinese mainland would be allowed; a naval blockade would be set up; and Chinese Nationalist forces would enter the battle; under these conditions it was determined that the atomic bomb could be used, if tactically appropriate.

Under the third scenario, the Chinese assault would continue but they would agree not to cross the 38th parallel, and the United Nations would accept an armistice agreement. The conditions of the armistice would require the withdrawal of North Korean guerillas from South Korea; and a United Nations commission should supervise the implementation of the armistice; then under these circumstances atomic weapons would not be used.

Although the first two scenarios were the ones that MacArthur advocated, it was the last scenario that actually happened in Korea from December 1950 through April 1951. And although the United States had contemplated using the atomic bomb in Korea, they did not employ them. President Truman did publicly threaten to use atomic weapons immediately after the Chinese intervention; however, about 45 days after the Chinese entered the war, the battlefield was again located close to the 38th parallel and had reached a tentative stalemate, and the atomic bomb had not yet been employed.

The United States reached its closest point of using nuclear weapons during the Korean War in April 1951, according to historian Bruce Cumings. At the end of March 1951, the Chinese had moved large numbers of infantry into Korea. According to Cumings, at that time the bomb loading pits at Kadena Air Base on Okinawa were made operational, and the bombs in those pits lacked only the nuclear cores to become deadly. On April 5, 1951, the Joint Chiefs of Staff ordered immediate retaliatory attacks using atomic weapons against Manchurian bases in the event that Chinese troops entered into battle or initiated bombing attacks from those Manchurian bases. Also on April 5, President Truman approved the transfer of nine Mark IV nuclear capsules to the Air Force's Ninth Bomber Group, and the President authorized their use against Chinese and North Korean targets. Historian Bruce Cumings reports, however, that this signed order was never sent because by that time the war had reached a stalemate, the Chinese and North Koreans did not escalate their offensive operations, and there was talk of peace negotiations starting.

The final decision not to use the atomic bomb was not due to the fact that the Chinese did not advance past the 38th parallel, but rather the decision was due to the pressure from United Nations allies, notably Great Britain and France, who warned that such an escalation using atomic weapons could lead to all out war with the Chinese and Soviet Russia in Asia and in Europe

# *REST AND RECUPERATION (R&R)*

Rest and Recuperation (R&R), is an army phrase that came out of the Korean War, meaning rest and recuperation from a combat zone. During the first year of the Korean War, the morale of the 8$^{th}$ Army troops was as low as it could get. One of the ways that the 8$^{th}$ Army in Korea attempted to raise morale was to start a new program of getting the troops off the front line, let them spend some time in Japan, and then send them back to their units. After a certain amount of time in a combat zone, these GIs would become eligible for a five day Rest and Recuperation leave in Japan. The program got started early in 1951, just five months after the start of the war, and it became an extremely important reason for the dramatic improvement in morale among the American enlisted men. Everyone was eligible for the program including American and United Nations soldiers, marines, airmen and sailors. However, it was the army infantry and artillery GIs who looked forward to R&R the most, and who benefited the most, because they were the ones who had to endure the extreme loneliness, exhaustion, severe weather conditions, and the danger of their combat assignments in Korea.

The change in environment from a foxhole in Korea to the bright lights of Tokyo and other Japanese cities, was a dream come true for a war weary GI. Rest and Recuperation was very quickly given other initials and wording by the soldiers, as they referred to R&R, as I&I, for intoxication and intercourse, or they referred to it as A&A, for ass and alcohol. A&A quickly became the most popular way to describe their five day leave in Japan, many of them saying that they needed two weeks back at their units to recuperate from their R&R leave. Regardless of the humor surrounding the terms for R&R, it became apparent very quickly that the program improved army morale substantially.

The men were selected for R&R based on their time spent in Korea, and once selected they were flown to Japan, usually Tokyo, where they were given billets in clubs for officers, non-commissioned officers, and enlisted men. Most of the men quickly left the army accommodations and took rooms at Japanese Inns catering to GIs on R&R. The night life in Tokyo offered everything that a young GI ever dreamed of, including superb Japanese food and drink, professional Japanese musical combos with pretty vocalists singing American pop songs, and beautiful Japanese girls who were willing to provide companionship for the American soldiers. The women were often beautiful, extremely polite, always well groomed, and with fastidious customs. The Japanese also ran official red-light districts that provided women and entertainment for every taste. Many of the Japanese girls and young women, except those in the red-light districts, were not prostitutes in the traditional sense; rather they were young women who were attracted to the excitement and the relative high life style that an American GI on R&R could offer. These Japanese women seldom strutted provocatively or "hustled" in a traditional manner; they stood shyly in the clubs where the GIs congregated, and they would respond positively if approached by an American GI who appealed to them. For the war weary soldiers from Korea, the five days in Japan under these exciting circumstances was a GI's fantasy come true.

WE ASKED THE FIRST SERGEANT FOR R AND R
AND ALL WE GOT WAS THE BIG HAR! HAR!
WE'RE MOVING ON, WE'RE MOVING ON
ASK FOR R AND R, GET THE BIG HAR! HAR!
WE'RE MOVING ON.

The proprietors of the Japanese Inns that catered to Americans on R&R leave, were always extremely polite and gracious. Very often the proprietor was a mature female, always called Mama-san by the GIs, who politely asked the soldiers to remove their shoes at the door; then he would be led to a scrupulously clean room with tatami mats on the floor with a spotless bed-roll. What followed would be bathing in a traditional Japanese hot tub, and then "resting and relaxing" with a beautiful Japanese young woman.

There was a language barrier, of course, between the Americans and the Japanese girls that did not diminish, however, the real feelings that sometimes arose between them. Many of the encounters between the GIs and their Japanese girlfriends, left deep and lasting emotions on both sides, and some couples were even able to arrange for marriage at a later time. The reconciliation between the Americans and the Japanese people also began to develop slowly during the years following the end of World War II, but it was the Korean War and the thousands of soldiers who briefly visited Japan on R&R, and met Japanese people in churches, hotels, clubs and other social gatherings, that slowly changed a mutual antagonism into a real affection between the two cultures. Any American who visited Japan under any circumstances after World War II, and even on those five day R&R leaves, came away from those visits with nothing but admiration for the Japanese people.

When the five days of R&R leave were over, the GIs were flown back to their combat assignments in Korea. They all brought back memories of their time spent in Japan, of their Japanese girl friends, and of the friends they made while there. Many of these soldiers also went back to their units with as much alcohol as they were allowed. When they got back to their outfits, they drank some of it and they sold some of it. In the early months of the Korean War, a bottle of whiskey sold for anywhere from $200. to $300. a bottle, and that was big money for soldiers back in 1950.

## *TROOP ROTATION*

During World War II, the United States Army had no plan to allow for the rotation of soldiers off the front line for short periods of time, to get a rest from the battlefield, before being sent back into combat. At that time the military kept the men in combat as long as necessary, and the GIs were replaced only on an individual basis if they became a casualty. The term "million dollar injury" was always used when a soldier was hit in combat but survived his injury, and was sent back to a hospital in the rear, or maybe even back to England, to recover from his wounds. These "million dollar injuries" often meant that the war was over for these GIs.

In Korea, a point system was started during the first year of the war. A total of 36 points were required for a soldier to earn a rotation back to the states. The point system was established to award four points for each month in a combat zone, three points were awarded for being located between regimental headquarters and emplaced batteries, and two points were given for rear echelon duty. The system was fair in that each man knew when he could return home; that is, an infantryman who survived nine months on the front line could expect to go home at the end of that time. However, the rotation policy had some drawbacks, especially as far as the officers were concerned. The term used in those early days in Korea for a soldier who had earned his points, was that he was a "short timer." And as soldiers became "short timers," many officers felt that these soldiers became more cautious in combat. These officers, who always sat back in Danger Rear, claimed that "short timers" would lack the necessary aggressiveness that was needed in combat. The officers, however, had no examples of this change in aggressiveness to support their claims. Another drawback offered by these officers, again without substantiation, was that this troop rotation destroyed unit cohesion. The officers felt that when the soldiers got "short," they began " making sure their own asses were protected during that time." Many officers felt that these "short timers" were more concerned about getting out of Korea alive, than they were about working as a member of a combat team.

A major concern of every enlisted man in Korea was to get out of that combat zone alive, and being a short timer never influenced their behavior regarding loyalty to their combat units. Officer complaints about the rotation plan set up for the troops, was just another example of how the army "caste system" works. In this case, officers rotation out of Korea was assured, whereas the officers were opposed to troop rotation for enlisted men, and felt that it should be abolished if once started.

Regardless of the complaints from officers about the troop rotation system, it went into effect in 1951 and stayed in effect until the end of the war. It should be noted that while many officers were quick to complain about a troop rotation program for enlisted men, these same officers made certain that they rotated out of Korea when their time was up.

# *BED CHECK CHARLIE*

Bed Check Charlie was the name the GIs gave to enemy airplanes that flew over American bases in Korea during the war. These aircraft were old, antique airplanes of two types: first, the YAK-18 Soviet built training planes. The YAK was a low-wing single engine aircraft with a cruising speed of 100 miles per hour, and a cruising radius of about 200 miles; and second, the PO-2, a Russian built wood and fabric bi-plane with a top speed of 110 miles per hour. Each of these aircraft was capable of carrying one or two small bombs.

These enemy planes were most often seen flying over American lines in the evening, usually about 11:00 or 11:30 p.m., when the lights in the army billets were turned off, and the troops were sacking out, which is where the name Bed Check Charlie came from. These YAK-18 and PO-2 aircraft would fly from North Korea into South Korea, flying low through the valleys to reduce radar detection. These planes also had to avoid the heavy cables that were strung from mountain top to mountain top by the North Koreans to prohibit American bombing runs from coming into the valleys.

Bed Check Charlie didn't fly into South Korea during rainy of foggy weather; they came in during the evening when the villages and army barracks were dark. These raids went on for the entire length of the Korean War, and one of the last reported raids was on June 3, 1953. That night Charlie came over Seoul with nine planes dropping bombs over the city, on American military bases, and one bomb actually dropped close to President Syngman Rhee's residence, although no one was injured. The last reported Bed Check Charlie was on June 16, 1953, just one month before the armistice was signed. That night a 15 plane Bed Check

Charlie raid succeeded in bombing a petroleum depot and supply base near Inchon, touching off 52,000 gallons of petroleum products, wiping out much of the supply base, and causing extensive damage. During these Bed Check Charlie attacks, the air raid sirens always went off, all the military went on high alert, all the search lights went on, the anti-aircraft batteries opened up, and everyone headed for bomb shelters or their foxholes.

The Air Force began attempting to shoot down Bed Check Charlie in 1951, but in order to do this they had to bring in slower planes to better attack the slow moving YAK-18s. The Navy F4U Corsair was brought in because of its slower speed; it was thought that the Corsair could better follow closely behind the YAK-18s and shoot them down. However, the American pilots had a difficult time estimating closure rates when they got behind a YAK or a PO-2. Many times the Corsair pilot would misjudge Charlie's slow speed and would end up ramming him sending both aircraft down in flames.

When the Americans got familiar with the slow speeds of Bed Check Charlie, they began shooting them down with ease, resulting in fewer bombing raids. On July 3, 1953, the last reported Charlie plane was shot down as it made a run over Seoul, after which there were no more reported raids by Bed Check Charlie.

# THE DOOLITTLE BOARD

The Doolittle Board was created by the Truman Administration in 1945, and its purpose was to iron out the inequities that existed between officers and enlisted men in the military. The Board was headed by General Jimmy Doolittle, and under his direction the Board made decisions and took subsequent actions, that had an effect on the structure of the military. The decisions and actions taken by the Board were in response to witness interviews, a survey of military personnel, and thousands of letters requested from members of the officer and enlisted ranks. The political purpose of the Doolittle Board was to attempt to eliminate the "caste system" in the army; a system that held officers in high esteem and constantly downgraded the enlisted ranks. One recommendation was to create an equalization between officers and enlisted men, essentially bridging the gap between shoulder rank and sleeve rank thereby improving the morale of enlisted personnel. The change in structure of the United States military was supposed to create a peacetime army that would encourage more young men to enlist.

The recommendations of the Doolittle Board were instituted in the United States military after 1946. It was right after World War II and both the civilian and military leadership had seen enough of war, so military discipline and training were relaxed. Soldiers serving in the United States and overseas at that time, felt as though they were on extended leaves. The Doolittle Board recommendations went into effect, and life for the enlisted man definitely improved. That is how the peacetime occupation army was structured in 1950 when North Korea invaded South Korea.

Then in July 1950, President Truman on the advice of his military advisors, ordered the U.S. Army 24th Division into Korea. What followed in Korea was a complete debacle for American forces during the first months of the war. The high level officers in Tokyo and at the Pentagon immediately began placing the blame for these defeats on the enlisted men in the war zone. These officers in Washington, D.C. and Tokyo were blaming everyone and everything except themselves; they blamed the Republic of Korea army, they blamed the segregated units, and they even blamed the recommendations made by the Doolittle Board, claiming that they destroyed military discipline, training, and fighting strength. The entire blame for what went wrong in Korea during the first year of the war, however, rests firmly on the shoulders of the Truman administration, General MacArthur, and their military advisors, who made blunder after miscalculated blunder in Korea in 1950 and 1951.

# KOREAN WAR REFUGEES

One of the major disasters of any war, one that does not get the attention it deserves, is the dislocation, suffering, and death of civilian refugees. During the Korea War, and especially during the first year of the war, North and South Korean refugees were almost always on the move. One week they would be moving south and the next week they would be moving north. The battlefield situation was so chaotic and disorganized that military commanders, not knowing who was an ally or an enemy, gave orders to their troops to take no prisoners. They ordered that if civilian refugees were seen approaching American lines, dressed in their customary long, white civilian garments, that the American soldiers were not to take any of these civilian refugees as prisoners. And so it was that during the first year of the Korean War, there were vast hordes of homeless peasants fleeing their homes and farms, brought into a tragic war they didn't understand, and very often they were shot by soldiers or strafed by American aircraft as they sought safety.

Starting in 2006 the government of South Korea established the Truth and Reconciliation Commission, whose mission is to determine the extent of the suffering of Korean civilians during the Korean War. The Korean researchers have examined recently declassified documents in the United States Archives and have concluded that the United States military did, in fact, indiscriminately kill thousands of Korean refugees and other civilians early in the Korean War. The Commission has documented more than 200 wartime accounts, based on hundreds of civilian petitions, that recount in great detail the bombing and strafing runs by U.S. pilots on South Korean refugee groups and villages in 1950 and 1951. The Commission goes on to claim that American pilots couldn't distinguish their South Korean civilian allies from the North Korean enemy soldiers, and that their bombing and strafing runs were indiscriminate and devastating, killing thousands of civilian refugees. Other declassified documents state that early in the war, American army ground commanders, fearing enemy infiltrators, had adopted a policy of shooting approaching refugees rather than taking them prisoner. It is reported that rumors spread among the troops regarding civilians approaching their lines with their hands in the air as if surrendering, only to open fire on the Americans when asked to approach. As a consequence of these rumors and of the policy ordered by the ground commanders, American GIs did not take prisoners under these battlefield conditions.

The Truth and Reconciliation Commission has been collecting evidence, reviewing declassified U.S. documents, and accumulating thousands of civilian petitions for the past two years. An example of refugee suffering during the war occurred at Yeongchun, South Korea in the winter of 1951. At that time civilian refugees were streaming over frozen roadways, looking for safety and with no place to go. There were hundreds of war refugees, laden with baggage on their backs, freezing and starving, and moving down mountain roads toward what they thought was the safety of American lines. These refugees were turned back at gunpoint and some were shot on sight. Within days, these civilian refugees and displaced villagers, who were crowded into hillside caves and shelters, came under waves of air attack by U.S. warplanes dropping bombs, napalm gel-fire canisters, and machine gun strafing. It is reported that more than 300 South Koreans died, many of them women and children, as they were trapped and burned in the smoke and flames; and it is further reported that if they attempted to flee, they were strafed by machine gun fire. One survivor stated that the people were moaning and screaming in the smoke and darkness, as many of them were being burned by the jellied napalm bombs. These napalm bombs, once delivered to the target, would spread quickly all over the ground and into the caves, virtually searching victims, burning everything in its path. The survivor who related this account was only a boy during this incident, and therefore couldn't understand the "fog of war" and the reason why the pilots couldn't tell civilians from North Korean troops. The Truth and Reconciliation Commission stated that in the last analysis, the U.S. military never took into consideration the terrible consequences that its massive bombing and napalm incineration operations would have on Korean civilians.

The United States government has been largely silent on the Commission's work. The U.S. Embassy in Seoul, Korea says that they have not been approached by the South Korean government about the Commission's findings. The National Assembly in Korea established a panel in 2007 to investigate the Commission's list of complaints, and also to investigate the claims that South Korea's authoritarian post-war regime led by Syngmon Rhee, ordered summary executions of suspected leftists in South Korea. And finally, the Korean Truth and Reconciliation Commission has recommended that the South Korean government seek victim's compensation from the United States government for the suffering and killing of civilian refugees during the first year of the war.

# *THE SOVIET UNION, THE UNITED NATIONS SECURITY COUNCIL, AND THE KOREAN WAR*

From the start of the Korean War, many in the United States and especially the right-wing hardliners in the Congress, were blaming the Soviet Union for everything that was going wrong in Korea. They were also blaming the Democratic Party and those who were moderate to liberal in their thinking, for being soft on Communism, and even using terms like appeasement and traitor for anyone who didn't see Communism as an evil, brutal economic system that was out for world domination. They also felt that the United States had abandoned Chang Kai-chek in the battle for mainland China, and saw that loss as the main reason for the war in Korea. The China Lobby was a powerful group in politics in those days, and their right-wing jingoistic pronouncements against China and Russia had a definite impact on political thinking in the United States.

When the North Koreans invaded South Korea in June 1950, the United States brought the issue of the North Korean invasion before the United Nations. The United States requested a United Nations condemnation of North Korea's invasion of South Korea. They also recommended the creation of a United Nations Security Force to halt the aggression. In 1950, the United Nations Security Council consisted of a total of five permanent member countries: the United States, Great Britain, France, China, and the Soviet Union. Also, at the outbreak of the Korean War there were two countries that claimed to represent China; namely, the Republic of China (Taiwan) and the People's Republic of China (Communist mainland China). The United States backed the Taiwanese government even though it represented a minute fraction of

Chinese people and land compared with the government on the mainland; and the Soviet Union backed the government on mainland China that controlled the entire country. In the voting that followed in the United Nations Security Council, the China seat was assigned to the Taiwanese government. As a result of this vote, the Soviet Ambassador Jacib Malik, was summoned back to Moscow for "consultations."

It was during the Russian absence from the Security Council that the vote to condemn North Korea was taken and quickly passed. It should be noted that North Korea always claimed that South Korea, under the leadership of Syngman Rhee and his desire to unify Korea under his command, had initiated the battle by invading across the 38$^{th}$ parallel into North Korea. Actually, since the country was divided in 1945, there had been many incursions over the DMZ by both sides resulting in hostilities. At any rate, there were two separate U.N. Security Council resolutions in June 1950, both condemning the actions of North Korea and supporting an active defense of South Korea. If the Soviet Union had been present for the Security Council vote, these U.N. resolutions would not have passed. In that event, with no Security Council resolution condemning North Korea, the United States would have been forced to act unilaterally, if at all. When Soviet Ambassador Malik returned to the United Nations in August 1950, there was nothing he could do to change or alter these resolutions, even though he was then appointed as president of the Security Council, replacing Norway's Arne Sunde.

Many historians claim that the Soviet Union's boycott at the Security Council proves that they neither ordered the Korean invasion, nor gave their permission, or were they even aware of the timing of the invasion. There are an equal number of historians, however, who claim that the Soviet boycott was nothing more than a strategy, a ruse to keep the Soviets from having to vote on these resolutions, thereby allowing them to informally abstain. Regardless of the intentions of the Soviet Union, the facts are that everything that followed in the chaos of the Korean War, benefited the Soviets to the great detriment of the United States. President Truman, following the belligerent advice of the China Lobby and other Congressional hardliners, committed the United States into what turned out to be a hopeless quagmire in Korea.

Throughout the war, Joseph Stalin through his U.N. Ammbassador Jacib Malik, continually asserted that the conflict, when it began, was purely and simply a civil war. Stalin further stated that the major powers, and especially the United States, should stay out of the conflict. History has shown, in the years following the end of the Korean War through documents obtained from Russia, China, and North Korea, that a Communist conspiracy to take over the world starting in Korea, was a myth. These documents have also shown that the Domino Theory, with Korea being the first domino to fall followed by Japan and then Hawaii, and then on to California, was also a myth.

Would the situation in Korea have been different if the Soviet Union had vetoed those U.N. resolutions? Would the United States have fought in Korea unilaterally? Could North Korea's aggression into South Korea been handled more effectively in the United Nations through diplomacy, followed if necessary, by military action? Regardless of how these questions are answered, the facts are that the Soviet Union stood by as the South Koreans and the United States fought the North Koreans and Chinese to a stalemate in a war that lasted three years, a war that served the Soviet Union's best interests, allowing the Soviets to focus their attention on matters in Western Europe, especially Germany.

As the Korean War dragged to a stalemate, Joesph Stalin and the Soviet Union remained on the sidelines, although Russia continually sent supplies, weapons, and aircraft to the Communists. The peace talks started in Korea in 1951, but it was only after Stalin's death in 1953, and the presidency of Dwight Eisenhower, that these talks became serious and reached a conclusion.

# KOREAN WAR ATROCITIES

When the Korean War reached a stalemate in 1951 and peace talks were underway, one of the main topics under discussion was the treatment of prisoners of war. Both sides maintained that their soldiers were mistreated after being captured; both sides claimed that their soldiers were tortured, starved, denied medical care, and sometimes executed while they were prisoners of war. Unfortunately, according to released documents from China, North Korea and the United States, it is now known that atrocities against prisoners of war were committed by both sides in the tragedy that was the Korean War.

Atrocities Against American Prisoners of War

In October 1953, in response to thousands of letters from parents, wives and relatives of servicemen who served in Korea during 1950 and 1951, who claimed that these servicemen were starved, beaten and tortured, the United States Senate appointed a special subcommittee to inquire into the nature and extent of Communist war crimes committed in Korea.

The first reports of war crimes committed by North Korean troops against United Nations military enlisted men became known as early as July 1950, just one month after the war began. When these reports reached General Douglas MacArthur he established a War Crimes Division whose purpose was to define and clarify what constituted a war crime, and then to investigate all reports of prisoner of war atrocities. A war crime was defined as "those acts committed by enemy nations which constitute violations of the laws of war, including contravention of treaties such as the Geneva Convention, as well as outrageous acts against persons or property committed in connection with military operations," as noted in the United States Senate Report #848 on Atrocities.

The Senate Report provided evidence of war crimes committed against American prisoners of war (POWs) during the first year of the war. The report states that American POWs who were not deliberately shot at time of capture or shortly after capture, were beaten, wounded, starved, denied medical care, humiliated before civilian groups, and forced to march long distances without benefit of food, water or clothing. The following cases represent the type of atrocities that were committed against American prisoners of war in Korea, according to the Senate Report.

1. Hill 303 Massacre

On August 14, 1950, a group of 26 American soldiers was captured by the North Koreans. The men were stripped of their combat boots and their hands were tied behind their backs. The second day after their capture, several more Americans were captured and added to their group. The total number of American POWs was now approximately 45. On the third day, all of the prisoners were led to a ravine, and without warning, while their hands were tied, they were shot. Amazingly, four Americans survived to tell their story.

2. The Sunchon Tunnel Massacre

In October 1950, at Pyongyang the capital of North Korea, at a time when the fall of the city appeared to be imminent, the North Koreans loaded 180 American POWs into open railway cars for transportation northward. These men had survived the Seoul to Pyongyang "death march" and were exhausted from the lack of food, water, and medical care. They rode in those open railway cars completely unprotected from the cold weather for four or five days, arriving at the Sunchon tunnel on October 30, 1950. Late in the afternoon, the Americans were led away from the railway cars toward nearby ravines where they were shot by North Korean soldiers, using Russian made machine guns.

These are two examples listed by the U.S. Senate Report on Atrocities. The Senate Report concluded that "two-thirds of all American POWs in Korea died due to war crimes."

Atrocities Alleged To Have Been Committed Against Communist POWs and Korean Civilians

A declassified United States Air Force document states "It is reported that large groups of civilians, either composed of or controlled by North Korean soldiers, are infiltrating United States positions. The Army has requested that we strafe all civilian refugee groups approaching our positions. To date we have complied with this army request."

Another document from the early days of the Korean War was sent to the U.S. State Department from United States Ambassador John J. Muccio in Seoul. This document from Ambassador Muccio informed the State Department that American soldiers had been ordered to shoot civilian refugees approaching their lines. This letter provided evidence that such a policy existed early in the Korean War, and was the first evidence that the order to fire on refugees was known to the upper ranks in the United States government. It has also been reported that American enlisted men were warned not to take enemy soldiers or civilian refugees as POWs; Another document uncovered by the Associated Press, showed a January 3, 1951 order by General Matthew Ridgway that gave combat units the authority to fire at civilians to halt their movement. These documents were all reported by July 1950, or by January 1951, as in the case of Ridgway's order.

In 1999, a Pulitzer Prize winning story by the Associated Press, documented the July 1950 massacre of 400 South Korean civilian refugees at No Gun Ri, a village about 100 miles southeast of Seoul, the South Korean capital. According to the report, these refugees were trying to escape the advancing North Korean forces by crossing over United States military lines. The officer in charge of the 7th Cavalry Regiment feared that North Korean soldiers disguised as civilians in long, white garments might be among these refugee groups. These officers ordered their troops not to take prisoners; they were to consider all refugees as potential enemy.

In late July 1950, this large group of South Korean civilian refugees was coming into the village of No Gun Ri, many of them were leading ox carts and carrying children on their backs. As the refugees approached No Gun Ri they were cut off by American soldiers and ordered off the road and onto parallel railroad tracks. The refugees were then ordered to follow the railroad tracks that led them under a concrete bridge. What happened under that concrete bridge cannot be reconstructed in full detail, although reports from Korean survivors and from ex-GIs who were at No Gun Ri, are in agreement that American planes suddenly began strafing the area and the large group of civilians huddled there. The ex-GIs, who were with the 7th Cavalry Regiment, said that they felt threatened by these refugees and saw them as the enemy, and that they opened fire on those civilians who survived the aerial strafing attack.

The tragedy at No Gun Ri and other alleged wartime cases are currently being investigated by the South Korean Truth and Reconciliation Commission. The Commission has documented several hundred alleged wartime incidents in which American bombing and strafing runs attacked large groups of refugees and other civilians early in the Korean War.

Unfortunately, in time of war, killing of the enemy who were either wounded or at times surrendering, was done by both sides. This was especially true in the early chaos of the Korean War. In the desperation of combat, particularly when there is no provision to care for the wounded and no troops to spare, and especially when the soldiers aren't sure who the enemy is, the men develop a "combat paranoia," and they begin to see everyone as the enemy, including civilians. To all soldiers, the difference between killing during combat and killing at any other time—is murder. But all soldiers also know that the definition of combat is subjective, and can vary widely depending on experience under fire and many other battlefield conditions. There is also the need for the military to maintain strict control over their defensive positions during combat. Anyone, civilian or military, who approaches a military defensive position during combat, does so at great peril.

Those are some of the facts regarding the battlefield conditions during the early months of the war. However, regarding the civilian refugee dilema, these peasants were fleeing their farms and homes to escape the violence, and they had no idea what was happening in their country. If the American GIs didn't know where they were in Korea or what they were doing there, and most of them didn't, the Korean peasants knew even less. They were all fleeing the battlefield violence and searching for safety; going south one day, then heading north the next day; one day waving an American flag, the next day waving a North Korean flag. For these civilian refugees, unarmed, carrying their children and belongings on their backs and on their oxen driven carts—their situation was a disaster from which it would take years to recover.

# *PRISONER OF WAR CAMPS*

In one of the North Korean prison camps established in 1951, more than 1500 prisoners, primarily Americans, are reported to have died in the early months of their captivity—from starvation, sickness, lack of medical treatment, and loss of morale. Regardless of these conditions, the Communist propaganda machine produced statements and pictures to the world press showing prisoners being well treated. Many prisoners, in response to promises of medical care, food, and the receipt of mail from home, signed documents describing their good treatment at the hands of the Chinese; many also signed statements admitting that they now realized the mistake they were making in "fighting for the immoral cause of American capitalism and imperialism." The Communists also allowed visits to the prison camps by left leaning correspondents who, on their return to their countries, claimed that the prisoners they interviewed were well fed and were not being indoctrinated.

Claims of mistreatment and torture of prisoners continued to be made by both sides right up until the armistice was signed in July 1953. To this day there are veterans of the Korean War who believe that in North Korea and Manchuria there are still American captives or their remains, who have never been disclosed as such by Chinese and North Korean officials.

On the United Nations side, the responsibility for the custody and treatment of North Korean and Chinese prisoners of war was taken over and conducted by the United States. The United States Army had stockades constructed near Pusan in August 1950, and at that time the stockades held about 1,000 North Korean Peoples Army captives. By the Spring of 1951 these stockades were not able to hold the increasing number of prisoners, so the Americans constructed large prison compounds on Koje-do, an island about 25 miles off the coast of Pusan. These prison camps were built to hold about 40,000 prisoners, but by the summer of 1951 these compounds held more than 150,000 North Korean and Chinese prisoners. These camps also held more than 100,000 refugees. To accommodate this number of prisoners and refugees, the Americans built an additional stockade at Cheju-do, a nearby island. The overcrowding in these stockades became so great during the Spring and early Summer of 1951, that the commandant of the prison and his staff completely lost control of the prisoners. Most of the guards were soldiers of the Republic of Korea army (South Korea) and they became involved with the prisoners in a thriving black market, dealing with cigarettes, drugs, whiskey, and prostitutes. Then by July 1951, all hell broke loose inside the island prison camp at Koje-do, when United Nations guards were attacked. This attack on prison guards was followed by mass rioting, which spread throughout the entire stockade. The United States Army sent in reinforcements but they couldn't stop the riots, beatings, and killing that took place inside the prison wire. By now the hard line North Korea Peoples Army prisoners were in full control of most of the prison, and the United Nations guards did not enter the prison compound by day or night unless under heavy guard. Many riots that occurred at the stockade resulted in the deaths of many of the prisoners. The stories of these riots spread outside the prison and onto the mainland, and within days the North Korean and Chinese delegations at Panmunjon were complaining bitterly to their U.S. and U.N. counterparts about the "barbaric" treatment of North Korean and Chinese prisoners of war.

    Brigadier General Dodd was dispatched to the Koje-do prison camp in an attempt to stop the prison rebellions. He established strict prison enforcement procedures, but the situation within the prison continued to worsen. In July, General Dodd and his deputy Lt. Colonel Rowen, entered the prison under guard in an attempt to mediate these problems, by establishing a prisoner committee. However, while these discussions were taking place, a militant group of prisoners seized General Dodd and held him as hostage. Several days later, after extensive negotiation, the prisoners agreed to release General Dodd, and finally in late summer the general was allowed to walk to his freedom. The terms of the agreement that allowed for General Dodd's release included the admission of responsibility by the General for the riots and many of the killings in the prison; the prisoners were promised humane treatment in the future; and the General agreed to establish a prisoner's representation group for further negotiations.

The prison mutinies at Koje was a public relations nightmare for the Americans, and a triumph for the Communists. They began to claim a moral ascendancy over the United States and United Nations command. For many days at Panmunjon, the treatment of prisoners on both sides, was high on the peace talk's agenda.

The United States Army held a Board of Inquiry regarding the conduct of General Dodd and his deputy that determined that General Dodd and his deputy were not to blame for the conditions at the prison and the riots that took place. However, because the U.S. Army felt humiliated by the whole situation at the prison and wanted to take disciplinary action, both officers were demoted one rank, and this verdict was upheld all the way back to Washington and agreed to by President Truman.

After the armistice was signed in 1953. Syngman Rhee released all anti-communist prisoners who were then allowed to settle in South Korea. The hard-line Communist prisoners who maintained their antagonism toward their American captors until the armistice was signed, were then repatriated and sent back to North Korea.

## THE NEVER AGAIN CLUB

During the first year of the Korean War, many officers and enlisted men had deep reservations about the United States military mission in Korea. Many of these men were combat veterans who had served in Asia during the second World War, and they had come away with a belief that American ground forces should never again get bogged down fighting an enemy on the mainland or islands of Asia. The fighting in World War II was universally looked upon by those in the military, officers and enlisted men, as being necessary, a war for a good cause. However, many of them did not have these same feelings about the war in Korea. These men had seen first hand the terrible logistical difficulties for American troops in Asia; they also knew that there was an inevitable deficit in manpower that always favored the enemy. These views were developed during World War II, and now five years later, the United States military found itself in an Asian war in Korea under even worse battlefield conditions than they had endured while they were fighting Japan in the Pacific.

The conditions in Korea, during the first months of the war, were at least as dangerous as those encountered in World War II. In Korea, the terrain, logistical problems, and weather were severe, and the manpower deficit was huge; and these officers and enlisted men had these views regarding Korea even before the Chinese entered the war, when the battlefield conditions went from bad to worse. Many of these men were sending letters back home in which they expressed these views. In recent years, these letters have been shared with historians and novelists who were writing about the Korean War. These letters expressly state that the reality of the war in Korea did, in fact, drastically dilute much of America's military strength, leaving the troops exposed to Asian warfare that none of these men were trained for, and against overwhelming enemy forces. Everyone, these letters maintain, was exhausted; there was no time to rest; no place to sleep or eat; and the enemy always chose the time and place to fight. The Americans would rather fight during the daytime; however, the North Koreans and Chinese always fought at night. That meant that the Americans never got a night off, they were always on the alert expecting an attack at any time, and many were afraid to go to sleep—never sure if they would ever wake up.

All of these concerns were prevalent among officers and enlisted men during the early months of the Korean War, and became the reason for a large number of military men to start a group that became known as the Never Again Club. These military men, both officers and enlisted rank, had a deep seated belief, developed from their combat experiences in World War II and Korea, that the United States military should never again fight on the Asian mainland, unless in response to an attack on their homeland. The Korean War ended in 1953, and in the next several years the United States was once again bogged down in another military quagmire on the Asian mainland in Vietnam. The members of the Never Again Club from World War II and Korea probably didn't have to fight in Vietnam, but the reasons these military men formed the Never Again Club were just as valid in Vietnam as they were in Korea.

PART VII
THE END OF THE KOREAN PIPELINE
CORPORAL DAVID HANSEN
SERGEANT JAMES FOLEY
TECHNICAL SERGEANT MICHAEL PARKER

## *CORPORAL DAVID HANSEN*

As Corporal Hansen was heading south after the rout at Unsan, from time to time he would see aircraft overhead, and some of these planes were dropping messages. Hansen picked up one of the leaflets and read it. The message to the American troops was to "get out of the area as best as you can," that they were on their own. Hansen already knew that it was every man for himself, as he wandered along aimlessly, always at night, hoping to meet friendly units. Several times Hansen walked or crawled past wounded soldiers, many of them pleading not to be left behind. "Don't leave me behind!" or "Don't leave me here for them."

For the next few days he was on the move, always after dark, while hiding out in caves during the day, getting very little sleep. He was out there in no man's land for over a week, alone, suffering from his wounds, and trying to work his way back to the American lines. He moved from house to house, he had nothing to eat, and he drank water from foul tasting streams. Finally he reached a dry river bed, and he stayed there and watched as tracer fire lit up the whole area. Hansen had no idea whether it was enemy fire or friendly fire, he was completely disoriented, and did not know which way to head.

One night he came upon a farm and slowly approached the farmhouse. As he was approaching, a Korean farmer showed up outside the barn holding a rifle. The farmer confronted Hansen, shouting at him in a language that he couldn't understand. As Hansen stood there he raised his arms in the air as if surrendering, or asking for help, but then as he began approaching across the field toward the barn, the Korean farmer, feeling threatened, opened fire and shot Corporal David Hansen several times in the chest. Hansen died almost immediately as he sank into the rice paddy. He was one of many Americans who died in the first devastating year of the Korean War. One of many thousands of Americans who would end up in Korean rice paddys during the fighting in 1950 and 1951.

Corporal Hansen died in Korea on November 3, 1950, just five months after the North Koreans crossed the 38$^{th}$ parallel and headed south toward Pusan. Hansen was at the battle of Unsan; referred to by some historians as the Warning at Unsan. He survived the initial encounter with the Chinese, but then lost his way as he tried to rejoin his unit, and other survivors of the Chinese attack. Before he reached the safety of his unit, he was shot by a North Korean farmer. Corporal Hansen's body was never recovered and he was listed by the U.S. Army as missing in action.

## *TECH SERGEANT MICHAEL PARKER*

The battles around the Iron Triangle in the Central Corridor of Korea started early in 1951 and lasted until the armistice was signed in 1953. The Iron Triangle was the hub of the enemy's strategic power and contained a road and rail network that ran from Manchuria to the Communist front lines. General Van Fleet ordered the 8th Army to advance and to set up a defensive perimeter just south of the base of the Triangle. Sergeant Parker was a radio operator with the 24th Division Artillery, and during this stalemate phase of the war the artillery became even more important. Under the new, more stationary battlefield conditions, the artillery was able to set up their big guns on a more permanent basis, and provide continual bombardment on the enemy lines. Parker's assignment as radio operator for Headquarters Company placed him in an important position. He maintained communication with the firing battalions and with the U.S. Air Force helicopters to obtain the enemy coordinates. He then sent out Morse code messages, in five letter code groups, to the firing battalions, who then began their artillery bombardments.

It was April 1951, during the rainy season, as the weather opened up and the rain poured down reducing the dirt roads to muddy quagmires. It became impossible for the supply vehicles to get munitions to the artillery, or to get weapon supplies to the troops on the front line. Close air support was not possible due to the weather, but the American medium bombers, using radar, were able to bomb the enemy rear areas almost around the clock. Sergeant Parker was unable to move his radio truck because of the road conditions, and was forced to remain in one position, leaving him vulnerable to enemy mortar and sniper attack. He became an easy target with his radio antennae reaching high into the sky above his radio vehicle. After several days of air bombardment, the enemy resistance slowed considerably, and General Van Fleet continued his attack. It was during this attack that Michael Parker was seriously injured when his radio vehicle took a direct hit during a mortar attack. He was air evacuated back to the army hospital in Ascom City where he spent several weeks recovering from his injuries. After he recovered from his wounds, Parker was assigned to the radio school in Ascom City as an instructor. For Sergeant Parker the war was over. The army life at Ascom City and at the radio school, was almost like pulling duty in Japan or Stateside. Ascom City was, in effect, a large army base not unlike one you would find in the United States, that had equipment, weapons, ammunition, and supplies. He joined the staff at the radio school as a Tech Sergeant, and taught Morse code and radio procedure to the men selected for this communication program. Michael Palmer was stationed at Ascom City for six months before being reassigned to the United States. After his discharge from the army, he went back to college to finish his education.

## *SERGEANT JAMES FOLEY*

Sergeant Foley was wounded in action at the battle of Kunuri, two days after the Chinese formally entered the Korean War, and just five months after the start of the war. Sergeant Foley was air evacuated to a mobile air service hospital (MASH) in Taegu, and then taken by plane to Japan.

For Sergeant Foley, whose wounds were severe and his recovery in doubt, the Korean War was over. Lying there in the hospital, Foley knew he was in bad shape by the way the doctors and nurses looked at him, and they had him on morphine 24 hours a day. The army surgeon spoke to Foley telling him, "Soldier, you've done your job. The war is over for you. You'll never have to go back." What the surgeon didn't tell Foley was that his chances for recovery were slim, that his chest wounds were severe and both his feet had been frozen. Sergeant Foley was groggy from the morphine and somewhat delirious most of the time, and as he went in and out of consciousness he thought of many things: he thought about the hills and mountains in Korea, and the heavy cables that were strung by the Chinese and North Koreans from one mountain top to another to keep U.S. airplanes and helicopters from flying into the valleys; he thought about the maze of tunnels dug by the North Koreans in the mountains and the ever present tunnel rim around every mountain in Korea; he thought about the American Air Force attacks that bombed the mountains and dropped the dreaded napalm fire bombs and he remembered watching as the jellied fire spread into the tunnels searching the enemy; he thought about pulling guard duty on top of those mountains and the orders he received about not taking any prisoners—they were told, "You'll see Gooks coming in dressed in long white civilian garments with their hands in the air as if surrendering, and if you start to take them as prisoners, they will open up those white garments and mow you down with Chinese burp guns"; he thought about the times he was on guard duty up in the mountains, and hearing sounds at night, and firing off rounds; he thought about life in the combat zone; he thought about life back at Danger Rear where you were lucky enough to get a shower and use a quartermaster latrine—that's a slit trench about eight feet long with a wooden plank with holes cut in it spread over the top of the trench and supported on both sides by oil drums for enlisted men to take their dump; he thought about knowing that you'd never get to sit next to an officer on a quartermaster latrine; he laughed about how the GIs would joke about the officers—saying that when an officer had to take a dump and he was in a forward location, he was air evacuated back to Japan so the sissy could take his dump in style; he thought about how there were no quartermaster latrines up front because they didn't have time to did a slit trench—the men took their entrenching tool and headed for the hills to take their dump,—all the while thinking about the rumors of GIs being shot or bayoneted by a North Korean, as the GI was crouched over with his fatigues down around his feet; he thought about how the troops washed when they were on the front line, with a steel helmet full of rationed cold water; he thought about how good that shower felt back at Danger Rear even though you had to wait in line with all those other bare-ass soldiers waiting their turn; he thought about never seeing an officer at the front, but seeing them all over the place at Danger Rear; he thought about GIs complaining that the only time they saw an officer of Colonel or above was when they staged war games, and called in air strikes dropping ordnance and napalm—the officers standing around in their pressed fatigues and shiny combat boots trying to look tough; he thought about his buddies from his outfit that had been killed in action; he thought about digging foxholes in Korea when the ground was frozen and covered with snow; he thought about a digging foxholes during the rainy season when the foxhole would be half filled with water before he finished digging; he thought about the freezing conditions in the winter and the pup tents set up to provide warmth, and heated by army issued space heaters fueled by gasoline that resulted in frequent fires; and finally he thought about his battle injuries and he wondered if he'd ever get back to the United States, if he'd ever get to see his family again.

Sergeant Foley died from his chest wounds one month after reaching the hospital, just one week after his right foot was amputated because of frost bite.

MR. TRUMAN SAYS IT'S THE DOMINO
FUCK THE DOMINO, IT'S TIME TO GO
WE'RE MOVING ON, WE'RE MOVING ON
CHINESE BURP GUNS BLOW, IT'S TIME TO GO
WE'RE MOVING ON.

# PART VIII
# EPILOGUE

The Korean War lasted three years, and was fought under very severe conditions that included harsh mountainous terrain and extreme fluctuations in temperatures. The American troops, who were first sent to Korea, were both untrained and poorly equipped for the battlefield and enemy they encountered. S.L.A. Marshall, a military historian, called Korea the nation's nastiest war. Years after the war ended, Secretary of State, Dean Acheson is reported to have said that if someone were to choose the worst possible location to fight a war, the unanimous choice would have been Korea. The Americans faced a formidable enemy in mountainous terrain, and weather conditions that included sub-freezing temperatures in the winter, humid sub-tropical summers, and a drenching rainy season. Some historians have also noted that once the United States committed American soldiers to fight and die in Korea, that the men sent there at the start of the war were actually ill-supplied and inexperienced cannon fodder, whose only purpose was to slow down the North Korean advance, and prevent a "Dunkirk-style" defeat at the hands of the Communists. All of these factors worked to neutralize the power of the Allied forces, and they especially affected the morale of the American troops. The conditions on the ground in the early months of the war also neutralized the effect of the American armored vehicles, tanks and artillery; and these same conditions favored the enemy and allowed them to develop an extensive tunnel system in the mountains to shelter themselves from Allied air power, artillery and napalm.

The Korean War started so abruptly, and events on the ground progressed so rapidly during the first weeks of the war, that the United States was completely unprepared to stage a proper response to the North Korean attack. To increase the size of the army, the Truman administration sent out a blanket recall of all reservists within weeks of the North Koreans crossing the 38th parallel, and the government then sent these men into battle in Korea as fast as they could get them there. Most of the soldiers were not even given furlough time to spend with their families at home, before being shipped overseas. The only official leave allowed was for so-called hardship leaves, that is, a death in the family or similar emergency. This mobilization and subsequent funneling of troops from civilian status to the front line in Korea in a matter of weeks, became known as the Korean Pipeline.

Most of these men being recalled had already served in World War II, many of them in combat, and they resented being sent to Korea to fight in a war on the other side of the world. On top of these resentments, these men also noted that even the President of the United States, who had ordered them into battle, was not referring to what was going on in Korea as a war. He downplayed the nature of the Korean War, as he addressed the American people, and referred to it as a "conflict," or as the Korean "police action."

In the early 1950s, when the Korean War started, television news reporting was in its infancy. The television news shows were brief and had little influence on public opinion, with the result that the news from Korea had little to no effect on the American people. At that time, very few books had been written about the Korean War, and the only movie linked to Korea was "The Manchurian Candidate," a story about an American prisoner of war in Korea who was brainwashed in a Chinese prison camp, and then sent to the United States programmed to assassinate an American presidential candidate. Because of the lack of media attention and inadequate television news coverage of the war, plus the fact that the Truman administration continually downplayed the nature of the conflict—the true brutality of the Korean War never penetrated the American psyche. The fact that between 400 to 500 Americans were being killed in action every week during the first nine months of the war in Korea, and that these casualties would eventually reach a total of 34,000 dead Americans, did not get through to the American people. They felt that the Korean War was a small, limited conflict on the other side of the world, and unless someone had a family member in Korea, there was a complete disconnect between the people at home and the soldiers who fought the war.

The American soldiers that fought in Korea during November and December 1950, and at the time when the Chinese army entered the war, were all heroes, most of whom were killed in action, and who never received the recognition that they deserved. All of these battles had a common base, made up of individual soldiers in squads and platoons. It was with this base, the enlisted men on the ground, that these battles were won or lost. The military estimates that for every man that reaches the front line of combat, there are nine soldiers backing him up. That backup goes from squad to platoon, to the regiment to the division, and finally to the army headquarters. In Korea, the outcome of each battle rested heavily on how long an isolated company of enlisted men could stand alone in defense of a solitary hill or ridgeline.

All wars may be the tragic end result of miscalculations or misinformation by the governments and high-level officers involved. If this is true, then Korea proved to be a war where almost every major decision was a miscalculation based on purposeful or inadvertent bad intelligence. First, the United States took Korea off their Asian Defense Perimeter, which in turn led the Soviets to give the go-ahead to the North Korean leaders to invade South Korea, confident that the Americans would not come in. Second, once in the conflict, the Americans miscalculated the North Korean troop strength and fighting ability. Third, the Americans paid no attention to military intelligence that warned of a Chinese intervention should United Nations forces go north of the 38th parallel and approach Manchuria. Fourth, and probably the greatest miscalculation of all, was the decision by General MacArthur, and agreed to by the Truman administration, to advance United States troops to the Yalu River after the victory at Inchon, all based on the assurances by MacArthur that the Chinese would not enter the war. This false confidence of General MacArthur, along with his bellicose statements about bombing Chinese installations in Manchuria and threatening the use of atomic weapons, certainly had a lot to do with the Chinese entering the war. This miscalculation, better stated as another bizarre campaign blunder by General MacArthur, ended up putting his troops in extreme danger by making them more vulnerable to enemy attack. In the weeks following the Chinese entry into the war, the Americans suffered thousands of dead and wounded, directly as a result of this MacArthur miscalculation.

Many of the Americans who fought in the Korean War, especially those who served during the first year of the war, felt that the country, that is, the people back home, had no idea of the brutal situation on the ground for the American soldiers in Korea. To many veterans of the Korean War, it seemed that no matter what they faced in Korea or what bravery they demonstrated, the people at home did not realize it, nor did they grant them the same status as they afforded the men who fought in previous wars or wars that followed. The Iraq War, for example, has lasted longer than World War II and has cost more than 4,000 American lives. By contrast, the Korean War lasted three years, and more than 34,000 Americans were killed in action along with 20,000 non-combat deaths. During the first year of the Korean War, more than 4,000 American enlisted men were killed in action every two months. Korea was a forgotten war back in the 1950s, and it remains known today as "The Forgotten War."

In July 1953, the Korean Armistice was signed and the war ended in a stalemate. Back in 1950, soon after the Chinese entered the war and the situation on the ground seemed bleak, the American troops were ready for a "tie" or a stalemate, and a stalemate was how the war actually ended some three years later. Although the Korean War, in more recent times, has achieved much more status as a hard fought conflict, in the years after the 1953 armistice the war was something of a dark spot in terms of military history. In recent years, and with the completion of the Korean War Memorial in Washington, D.C., the war is now almost always noted when referring to conflicts that the United States can be proud of.

In 1953, when the war ended in stalemate, the American public and the military did not look upon the outcome of the Korean war as a victory. The Chinese, on the other hand, were proud of their participation, and what they saw as their success in Korea. They also felt that they had no alternative but to enter the war, as United Nations forces approached the Manchurian border. By entering the war and then forcing the United Nations forces to withdraw back to the 38$^{th}$ parallel, and then fighting to a stalemate, the Chinese felt as if they had achieved their objectives, and that they had defeated the most powerful nation in the world, a nation that had just defeated Germany and Japan.

What has happened in South Korea in the years after the war has been impressive and dramatic. The nation has stabilized and developed economically, industrially, and militarily. For the Americans who fought in Korea, the success of the South Korean nation has brought a sense of validation of their efforts. They were proud of having served in Korea, and now can look on as South Korea develops into a highly productive and successful democracy.

# PART IX
# WEAPONS USED DURING THE KOREAN WAR

### The M-1/Garand
*A semi-automatic rifle, gas operated; loads an eight-round .30 - caliber clip, and weighs 9.5 pounds.*

### The Carbine .30 Caliber
*A full automatic weapon that fires a .30 caliber bullet, and weighs 6 pounds. The carbine has far less range than the M1 rifle with less stopping power.*

### Browning Automatic Rifle (BAR)
*A full automatic weapon that can be operated one shot at a time. When on full automatic the BAR will put out up to 500 .30 caliber rounds per minute. The BAR weighs 16 pounds and may be fired from the hip, shoulder or bipod.*

### Infantry Mortars
*The mortar is a simple sealed-breech tube supported by a base plate, and comes in three sizes: 60-mm, 81-mm, and 4.2 inch. The mortar is useful for lobbing shells at a high angle at targets that are protected by hills, ridge lines or some other obstacle. The projectile is dropped into the muzzle of the mortar and has a range up to 4,000 yards.*

### 3.5 Bazooka
*The inside diameter of the launcher is 3.5 inches. The bazooka fires an 8.5 pound rocket which contains a hollow shaped charge that can be concentrated on a small area or target. The large rocket has a maximum range of several hundred yards, but to be effective against medium tanks the bazooka should be within 70 yards or less of the target. The 3.5 bazooka is usually handled by a two-man team.*

### Wheeled Vehicle Mounted With Quad-50

The Quad-50 is a vehicle with four mounted .50 caliber Browning machine guns. These weapons may be fired singly or as a unit. In Korea, the Quad-50s were a main support of the infantry line. The battery fire of the Quad-50 is overpowering and brackets the target. For the enemy caught in the fire of a Quad-50 there seems to be no escape and it was the No. I demoralizer of enemy infantry in Korea.

### The Browning light .30-caliber Machine Gun (LMG)

The Browning LMG is air-cooled and can fire up to 500 rounds per minute. It has a metal shoulder stock, pistol grip, and bipod. The LMG weighs slightly more than 32 pounds unloaded, and is an infantry weapon that is effective in hill and ridgeline fighting.

### The Browning heavy .30-caliber Machine Gun (HMG)

The Browning HMG is water cooled, fought from a tripod, and can fire up to 600 rounds per minute. The water cooling system of the HMG allows it to sustain action for longer periods of time than the LMG, and its effective range is three times that of the LMG.

### The Browning .50-caliber Machine Gun

This weapon has a heavy barrel which allows it to fire long bursts of up to 600 rounds per minute. It weighs 82 pounds and is usually mounted on a transport vehicle.